Orlando
Tips for Brits

CATHERINE HARRIOTT

Congratulations on winning !

Catherine Harriott

www.CatherineHarriott.com

PUBLISHED BY LIBRARY STAMP

PLEASE NOTE
At time of writing, details, including addresses, phone numbers and web links
were correct, however, be aware these are subject to change and the reader should
check for themselves.

No advertising is used in this book and the writer does not endorse any company.

IMPORTANT
ESTA: To travel to the United States you must sign-up for the Electronic System
Travel Authorisation, known as ESTA, which allows you to travel under the Visa
Waiver Programme. This replaces the old Visa Waiver green form you used to fill
out on the plane. Your ESTA number lasts for two years or until your passport
expires. You must fill out the ESTA form online at: https://esta.cbp.dhs.gov/esta

Also, please ensure your passport is a biometric one (also known as an e-passport).

TO MY FAMILY

Who happily enjoy everything in Orlando with me.

CONTENTS

WHY ANOTHER GUIDE TO ORLANDO?

'There are no foreign lands. It is the traveller only who is foreign.'

Robert Louis Stevenson

You'll find plenty of guides to Orlando and Florida, including the excellent *Brit Guide to Orlando,* so why, then, have I written another?

Well, the idea for this book hatched in a make-a-plan-on-a-napkin moment when I was sitting in a restaurant in Orlando, and I overheard a British visitor struggling to make herself understood with the waitress. She was trying to order a lemonade. Obviously jet-lagged, this poor lady was getting more and more stressed and frustrated as she kept repeating herself because she didn't realise she was asking for the wrong thing. Or the right thing, just with the wrong word. She should have been asking for a Sprite or 7-Up, as lemonade in America is always the old-style, non-fizzy drink made with real lemons and sugar.

On that same day, I bumped into two visitors at the supermarket who couldn't work out the difference between American dish washer and dish soap. I had visions of their holiday [vacation*] villa's dishwasher machine foaming up volcano-like when they poured in the wrong soap, and then being charged for an expensive plumber callout by their rental agency.

These two chance meetings got me thinking about the whole Orlando visitor experience. I wondered how other Brits were doing, coping with the language and cultural differences, being thrown into a completely new environment, negotiating unfamiliar roads, striving to cram in everything at a theme park in the heat and humidity while perhaps juggling budgeting concerns and handling family squabbles. It all mounts up and it's enough to ruin your holiday mood. That's why I wrote this guide, to help you, the British visitor to Orlando, plan and enjoy your visit to the fullest.

Catherine Harriott

---

*Words in square brackets throughout this book are the American translation.

ALSO BY CATHERINE HARRIOTT

Missing in Time:
Sally Soforth and the Secret Portal

Sally's Movie Diary:
A Companion to Missing in Time

1 ORLANDO'S BACK STORY

There's always something new to do in Orlando.

Always.

No matter what the state of the economy is, someone, somewhere, is opening a new attraction, restaurant, shop, hotel or ride. It's wonderful. And it means that visitors are never bored.

But it wasn't always like that.

For 14,000 years (give or take a few thousand, depending on human habitation evidence) the first Native Americans occupied the land. They came during an ice age, travelling across a land bridge called Beringia – a thousand-mile stretch between glaciers – from Eastern Asia to North America, arriving eventually in Florida. These were nomadic people. But with the rising of sea levels and the end of the ice age, they settled into tribes, living in villages, growing squashes, beans and corn, and fishing the waters.

Then, five hundred years ago, the first Europeans arrived in Florida: the Spanish followed by the English. They brought with them their old-world attitudes and diseases that, over the course of three hundred years, wiped out at least 100,000 Native Americans, leaving a handful to survive.

By the 1800's, the area was filled with cowboys, cattle ranches and saloons, and Orlando was known as the Wild South.

With the advent of the railway in the 1880's, the economy took an upswing, and farms growing citrus fruit flourished. However, except for the downtown city area, Greater Orlando was still a backwater full of swamps, mosquitoes and alligators.

ORANGE COUNTY REGIONAL HISTORY CENTER*
Location: Downtown Orlando
65 E. Central Blvd., Orlando, 32801
(Parking Garage Address: 112 E. Central Blvd.)
Tel: 407-836-8500 www.TheHistoryCenter.org

In the early part of the 1900's, a trickle of tourists from wintery climes started to escape to Florida, heading for the coastline. They were known as Tin Can Tourists because of the Model-T Fords (nickname: Tin Lizzie) they drove and the cans of food they packed in their boots [trunks]. After World War II, these same tourists came back to Florida towing caravans [trailers] behind their cars.

TIP Florida is in the southern states of North America. Orlando is in Central Florida.

*Please note American spelling of names throughout.

Visitors had little to do except perhaps visit Gatorland to see wild alligators up close and personal (operating since 1949 and still open). Maybe they stayed at the Wigwam Village Motor Lodge, tucked inside the orange groves that once grew along Orange Blossom Trail.

Wigwam Village Motor Lodge 1948

Or, perhaps they'd pass through on their way to the Weeki Wachee Springs to see 'live mermaids' swimming in the clear river; another attraction still open today (go to: OFF THE THEME PARK TRACK chapter for more details on both Gatorland, page 141, and Weeki Wachee Springs, page 135). But apart from these places, Orlando wasn't much of a holiday destination.

Then Walt Disney came to town – and everything changed.

IT ALL STARTED WITH A MOUSE

It was 1964, and the great Mickey Mouse creator and animator, Walt Disney, who was already running a successful theme park in California (Disneyland) decided he wanted to build a second park (Disney World) right here in the Sunshine State.

To prevent a sudden spike in land prices that his interest would invite, Walt sent his agents to scout Central Florida for farms and cattle ranches to snap up. They secretly purchased Disney's first Floridian land for a bargain $183 an acre, and by 1971, Walt had purchased roughly 30,000 acres, and Magic Kingdom (107 acres), Orlando's first theme park, was ready to open.

Today, Walt Disney World comprises of four theme parks, two water parks, a campsite, and 25 resorts operated by Disney, covering roughly an area of 45 square miles, about the size of Jersey in the Channel Islands.

Disney has attracted other profitable tourist investments – hotels, restaurants, service industries – and other theme parks such as Universal Studios and Sea World. In other words, everything is here because of Walt Disney, and Orlando is known as the town the Mouse built.

A SLICE OF ORLANDO LIFE

In the last twenty-five years, the population of Greater Orlando has tripled.

Yes, tripled.

Americans and immigrants are attracted here by the sunshine, relatively affordable housing, and employment. Roughly twenty-five percent of the local population is Hispanic (Spanish-American), originating from countries such as Cuba, Mexico and Puerto Rica. Most of the population live in apartments or small homes with pools in look-a-like housing estates called sub-divisions. But to discover a slice of upscale American life, Winter Park, with its majestic oak trees draped in Spanish moss, is a good place to start. You can take the scenic boat tour along the lakes and canals, viewing mansions and homes with traditional shutters and porches (ScenicBoatTours.com).

Or, for something completely different, you could visit the Disney-designed town of Celebration located off Highway 192 in Kissimmee.

Note: Go to: All-American Town in OFF THE THEME PARK TRACK chapter on page 143 for more information on Celebration.

The houses in Celebration also have shutters and porches, and you'll find restaurants, gift and clothes shops and a state of the art hospital that feels and looks more like a hotel than a medical facility. The town was designed with walking in mind, a pleasant change in vehicle-first America. The thing is, to go and explore the region with the help of this book, and you'll never know what you'll discover.

Homes in Celebration, Florida

FLORIDA TIMELINE

1513 Juan Ponce de Leon, a Spanish explorer, landed in St. Augustine and named the New World, La Florida, after the Spanish Easter celebration Pascua Florida (feast of flowers). He was killed by Native Americans while trying to set up a colony.

1565 The Spanish established Florida's first permanent settlement in St. Augustine.

Ponce de Leon

1586 Sir Francis Drake and the English arrived in Florida. However, unable to gain control of the wooden Spanish fort, they left.

1668 After English buccaneers attacked St. Augustine, the Spanish built a stone fort, Castillo de San Marcos, which still stands today.

Sir Francis Drake

1702 In 1702 (and in 1740) the British tried to capture St. Augustine but again were unsuccessful.

1763 Finally, the Brits won control of Florida by Peace Treaty – in exchange for Havana, Cuba – and Spain evacuated St. Augustine. British rule only lasted twenty years, though, before Spain, once again, won control.

1821 Spain ceded Florida to the now independent United States of America. But a US congress member declared Florida, 'a land of swamps, of quagmires, of frogs and alligators and mosquitoes.' A place 'no man would immigrate into, no, not from Hell itself.'

The US government fought many land wars with Native Americans. But it cost the government $40M just to relocate 3,000 and kill 1,500 (300 escaped to the swampy Everglades). During these wars the Seminole war leader, Osceola, whose father was actually British, is remembered for his tenacity and bravery, and today Osceola County is named after him.

Osceola

1883 Much of Florida now had railways and the first electric lighting was installed at Jacksonville Hotel.

1964 Walt Disney bought his first farm acres in Central Florida for $183 an acre, and the rest, as they say, is history.

2 HOTEL TIPS

This chapter will guide you into making your hotel choice based on area, amenities, budget, and convenience to theme parks. And to save confusion, you'll discover American hotel terms and differences, as well as a sample of resorts to choose from.

TIP The most inexpensive Disney hotels to stay at are Pop Century, Allstars Sports, Music and Movies, and the Art of Animation, which were all built with Brits in mind.

Note: Many British families opt for a villa or apartment rental, so for details and tips, go to next chapter: HOLIDAY HOME TIPS on page 23.

CHOOSING YOUR HOTEL

The hotel location you choose depends on . . .
a) How close you want to be to a theme park.
b) Whether you are hiring [renting] a car or not.
c) Whether you're looking for the party scene, family scene, or peace and tranquillity.

What type of hotel you choose depends on . . .
a) Your budget.
b) How many amenities you want.
c) Whether you have children or not.

Area: If you won't be hiring [renting] a car then look to stay as close to a theme park or hotel with shuttles. Three areas: Lake Buena Vista, the town of Kissimmee, and International Drive are all convenient areas close to the parks. Hotels usually provide the mileage distance to theme parks. If not, then ask. If they do offer a shuttle bus, check schedules and exactly which parks they service, or if there is a cost involved. Something to bear in mind at the end of a long day: shuttle buses can take a long time to complete their full stop-off routes.

Chains: When choosing a hotel, Americans usually stick to either theme-park hotels or hotel chains for good reason. They are usually dependable and have a good level of amenities, cleanliness and up-to-date rooms. Chains such as: Marriott, Doubletree, Best Western, Hyatt, Quality Inns, Wyndham, Hilton, Embassy Suites, Hampton Inns, Sheraton, Residence Inns, are all good bets.

Online Research: When you've narrowed a list of possible places to stay, research them on sites such as TripAdvisor.com that post reviews and candid guest photographs. But don't make a decision based on one review you read. Look to see a trend. For instance, if several people are saying the hotel is not suitable for children, then take notice. And what would concern some – such as no 24-hour room service – may not trouble you.

Occasionally, you'll read a review totally out of sync with the rest. It's probably a false one made by someone with a personal grudge (or, sadly, from a competitor).

TIP Americans often give tougher online hotel reviews than Europeans – something to bear in mind.

Prices: When comparing hotel prices beware of false economy. Do room rates include all taxes and resort fees? Are there other charges such as valet parking fees? Florida hotels and other accommodations charge between 11 and 13 percent total taxes, per room, per night.

If you're thinking of staying outside the direct theme-park area and have to pay for expensive taxies because you're not hiring [renting] a car, you may save money staying closer, after all.

Of course, everyone knows packages are more cost effective than booking hotels, flights and transport separately. But do you really need that dining plan with full breakfast or dinner? It may be cheaper just to eat outside the hotel or to have a room with a fridge and stock it with breakfast items, snacks or leftovers from those huge American restaurant meals. Or you can book a room with a kitchen.

And because they don't always tell you, be sure to ask if the hotel or tour company you're booking with have any special offers that could save you money or at least upgrade you to a better room. (For a sample of room rates, go to the end of this chapter, page 17.)

TIP If you've hired [rented] a vehicle, don't forget to factor in nightly parking charges when deciding on a hotel to stay.

THEME PARK HOTELS

Many people prefer to stay at a theme park hotel or resort, and why not, they are often magical places to stay.

Note: For latest prices and packages, go to either Disney or Universal web addresses below.

 **DISNEY HOTELS**

https://DisneyWorld.disney.go.com/resorts
Disney Resort Hotel Reservations Telephone Nos.
US: 407-939-1936
UK: 0870-242-4900

DISNEY'S MYMAGIC+

Disney resort guests and annual passholders wear the MagicBand wristband to use for their room key, park tickets, fastpass+ and reservations.

For more details, go to website:
MyDisneyExperience.com

Disney Hotel TIP: Disney hotel guests can arrive one-hour prior and up to two-hours after a park closes. Called EXTRA MAGIC HOURS, each day a different park stays open longer. Parking is free.

DISNEY HOTELS CLOSE TO MAGIC KINGDOM
Disney's Grand Floridian Resort & Spa
Disney's Contemporary Resort
Disney's Polynesian Village Resort
Disney's Fort Wilderness Resort & Campground

DISNEY HOTELS CLOSE TO EPCOT
Disney's Beach Club Resort
Disney's BoardWalk Inn
Disney's Beach Club Villas
Disney's BoardWalk Villas
Disney's Caribbean Beach Resort
Disney's Yacht Club Resort
Disney World Dolphin and Disney World Swan

DISNEY HOTELS CLOSE TO HOLLYWOOD STUDIOS
Art of Animation Resort

DISNEY HOTELS CLOSE TO ANIMAL KINGDOM
Disney's Animal Kingdom Lodge
Disney's Coronado Springs Resort
Disney's Value Resorts: Pop Century Resort, All-Star Movie Resort,
All-Star Music Resort, All-Star Sports Resort

DISNEY HOTELS WITH KITCHEN-IN-ROOM/FAMILY SUITES
Bay Lake Tower at Disney's Contemporary Resort
The Villas at Disney's Beach Club
Disney's Fort Wilderness Resort and Campground
The Villas at Disney's BoardWalk Resort
Disney's Saratoga Springs Resort
Disney's Old Key West Resort
The Villas at Disney's Wilderness Lodge

Disney Luggage Delivery: Disney resorts offer the free express service to and from Orlando International Airport. Book online or call the same number you booked your reservation. Once your luggage has cleared Customs, you leave it at the Disney Magical Express drop off. Disney then takes your luggage to your hotel room while you travel in one of their air-conditioned coaches [buses]. It can take up to three hours for your luggage to arrive, so keep anything you need immediately to hand. Once at a Disney resort you can shuttle to theme parks by bus, monorail or boat – all complementary services.

DISNEY HOTELS WITH STOPS ON THE FREE
MONORAIL TRACK TO MAGIC KINGDOM*

1. Contemporary
2. Grand Floridian
3. Polynesian

*You can also get to EPCOT by transferring at the monorail Main Ticket Centre.

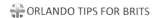

FREE STUFF WHEN STAYING AT DISNEY HOTELS
Free theme-park parking
Free coaches [buses] and ferries
Free airport shuttles
Free extra time at the theme parks
Free MyMagic+ enrolment: www.MyDisneyExperience.com

Note: For details of Disney Dining, go to page 102 in the DINING OUT TIPS chapter.

TIP For camping, there's Disney's Fort Wilderness Resort and Campground, the most inexpensive Disney place to stay.

UNIVERSAL HOTELS

www.UniversalOrlando.com

UNIVERSAL HOTELS CLOSE TO UNIVERSAL STUDIOS AND ISLANDS OF ADVENTURE:

Loews Portofino Bay Hotel	Hard Rock Hotel	Loews Royal Pacific Resort	Cabana Bay Beach Resort
5601 Universal Blvd. Orlando 32819 Tel: 407-503-1000	5800 Universal Blvd. Orlando 32819 Tel: 407-503-ROCK (2000)	6300 Hollywood Way Orlando 32819 Tel: 407-503-3000	6550 Adventure Way Orlando 32819 Tel: 407-503-4000

Note: Universal also partner with other hotels in Orlando and list them on their website (UniversalOrlando.com); a good way to ensure a degree of quality.

UNIVERSAL HOTELS WITH KITCHEN-IN-ROOM
Cabana Bay Beach Resort

Universal Hotel TIP: If you're staying at a Universal hotel, then you'll receive a pass for unlimited Express Ride Access in the park. Ask at your hotel reception [lobby] for details.

 # HOTEL AMENITIES

Floridian hotels usually have spacious and modern air-conditioned, ensuite rooms with comfortable beds. Room rates in Orlando are competitive and, apart from taxes that add between 11-13 percent to each room per night, many of this long list of amenities are included in the room rate:

- Shuttle buses between airport and theme parks.
- Free Breakfasts (usually continental but not always).
- Children's meals.
- Internet access.
- US newspapers delivered to your door.
- Parking and/or valet service (but check to see if there's a parking charge).
- In-room coffee and tea. (Most American hotels provide coffee/tea-making machines. If you would like a kettle, ask at front desk if they will provide one).
- Free local calls (but watch out for hefty long-distance charges).
- Use of business centres.
- Fitness rooms.
- Hot tubs and pools.
- Children free in room.
- Late check outs (according to availability).

Ice, Ice, Baby: Florida hotels all have ice machines (often on every floor) for filling ice buckets provided in your room – handy for drinks or keeping a bottle of wine cool.

TIP If you overheat in the Florida sun, pack ice in a hand towel and fold the towel round your neck for a few minutes of cool relief.

Mini Bars and Movies: In-room stocked mini bars are convenient but can be costly. Before helping yourself, read the pricelist to see you are not paying $5 for a bag of peanuts. Hotels usually offer in-room films [movies] for a charge that will be placed on your bill.

Guest Services: Most large hotels have a concierge or guest services desk; don't be shy about using them. You can either phone the concierge from your room for information on theme parks, restaurants, tours, shows, or you can go to their desk in the reception area [lobby]. No need to tip unless someone's gone to a lot of trouble, such as arranging theatre tickets. Watch out, though, some hotel Guest Services try to offer you tours of time-share properties in exchange for theme park tickets. Something to be avoided.

CHECKING IN/CHECKING OUT

Checking In: As with British hotels, you check in at the front desk of the reception [lobby] (the receptionist is called a desk clerk). Have your room confirmation details with you. Saves a lot of hassle if the hotel loses a record of your booking.

Types of Bed:

A single bed is called a TWIN

A small double bed is called a QUEEN

A large double bed is called a KING

Types of Room:

STANDARD (still usually good quality)

LUXURY (usually bigger, in the best location)

SUITES (often with separate bedrooms)

EFFICIENCY SUITES OR FAMILY ROOMS (with kitchenettes)

TWIN ROOMS (with two large single beds)

DOUBLE ROOMS (with one double bed)

PENTHOUSE (same as UK, top floor and luxury)

Extra Beds: Do you need a bed settee? Then ask for a sofa bed or a rollaway. Do you need a baby's cot? If so, ask for a crib.

Smoking: Make sure you have a non-smoking room or a smoking room; whichever is your preference, although most Orlando hotels these days are fully non-smoking.

ORLANDO HOTELS WITH SPA FACILITIES
Walt Disney Swan and Dolphin
Ritz-Carlton Orlando
Disney's Saratoga Springs
Gaylord Palms Resort
Universal's Portofino Bay Hotel
Hyatt Regency Grand Cypress

Card Swipe: At check-in you'll be asked for your credit/debit card for the receptionist [desk clerk] to swipe, so that a hold may be put on your card to cover your nightly room rate, and also so any extra charges, incidentals, meals or room service charges can be added to your card before departure. For this reason, it's a good idea not to use your debit card, so that all your holiday funds won't be tied up. If you're concerned, ask how much is going to be blocked. (When you check out, if you pay your final bill with another card, ask for the hold to be taken off the card you used to check in with.)

Extra Keys: You can ask for extra door key cards for your children if you need them.

Air-con: All rooms have their own bathrooms and lovely air-conditioning (that can be switched over to heat if necessary). Turn off the air-conditioning when you leave your room, although the housekeeper may switch it back on for your return. For efficiency, don't keep the balcony door open while running air-conditioning.

Too Close to the Lift [Elevator]?: If you're unhappy with your room, then ask to be moved. Most American hotels want to provide the best possible service for their guests, and they will usually try to accommodate you. Don't forget, if you are disturbed in the night by noisy guests, complain straight away to the night manager. Never suffer in silence. That's what they're there for!

TIP In American lifts [elevators] the ground floor is called the FIRST FLOOR. So if the hotel receptionist [desk clerk] tells you your room is on the first floor, don't take the lift [elevator].

Checking Out: If you'd prefer a late check out (say 1 or 2 PM) call front desk and see if that's possible. Or, if your flight is a late one, you can always leave your bags with front desk and enjoy a few hours of extra holiday [vacation] time. Remember, there are always towels at the pool if you want to go swimming.

Bags: If a porter [doorman or bellhop] helps carry your bags, then it is usual to tip him a couple of dollars.

Help: If you need assistance with bags, call down to front desk for a porter [bellhop]. If you're in a hurry, you can usually check out electronically through a channel on your TV. Otherwise, go to front desk. Read the bill to see if you agree with the charges.

You Left WHAT?: Before leaving your room, do a quick check to see if you've forgotten anything. Don't forget to look in bed sheets, under beds and behind curtains, especially if you have children who leave toys in these areas. Also check for mobile [cell] phone chargers or any other plugged-in items. Check for items in safes, drawers, the bathroom (don't forget to peek around at the door hook) and wardrobes [closets]. This may sound obvious but hotels are always returning items left behind by guests.

SAMPLE OF HOTELS (Not Theme Park)

Greater Orlando has hundreds of hotels and resorts. Below is a good sample just to give you an idea of what's available, but please do your own research to see if they suit. Or get a recommendation from a friend, relative or trusted travel agent. (Go to: THEME PARK HOTELS on page 9 for Disney and Universal hotels and resorts).

Note: The room rates on the following pages are approximate and often can be found cheaper or more expensive, depending on booking agent, website, season or sale rates.

TIP When booking or deciding to book, don't forget to ask about extra daily charges, such as taxes and resort fees, parking/valet service, and maid service.

$$$ LUXURY (OVER $200 PER ROOM, PER NIGHT)

Ritz-Carlton Orlando Grande Lakes
Sat Nav Address: 4012 Central Florida Parkway, Orlando, 32837
Tel: 407-206-2400
www.RitzCarlton.com
Location: 10 miles from Disney

The level of accommodation at the Ritz-Carlton Orlando Grande Lakes is what you'd expect from a Ritz hotel – spacious rooms, attentive service, convenience to highways. A bonus of this hotel is the shared use of facilities with the Marriott next door, including their Lazy River pool.

Waldorf Astoria Orlando
Sat Nat Address: 14200 Bonnet Creek Resort Lane, Orlando, 32821
Tel: 407-597-5500
www.WaldorfAstoriaOrlando.com
Location: Disney Springs, Lake Buena Vista

Fourteen-floor hotel with all the amenities of a luxury resort, such as spa, golf course and four pools. Rooms include plush beds, 42" TVs and marble bathrooms.

Gaylord Palms Resort (Marriott)
Sat Nav Address: 6000 W. Osceola Pkwy., Kissimmee, 34746
UK Tel: 00800-1927-1927, US Tel: 407-586-0000
www.marriott.com/hotels/travel/mcogp-gaylord-palms
Location: Close to town of Celebration

This unusual hotel and convention centre has over 1,400 rooms, many overlooking their famous incredible tropical atrium. Fine dining restaurants are top class with wonderful views. Note: This is a fully non-smoking hotel.

$$ MID-PRICED ($150 AND UP, PER ROOM, PER NIGHT)

Holiday Inn, Orlando Disney Springs
Sat Nav Address: 1805 Hotel Plaza Blvd, Lake Buena Vista,
Orlando, 32830
Tel: 407-828-8888
www.HolidayInn.com
Location: Close to Disney Springs
(with shuttle buses to Disney theme parks)

Clean, spacious rooms in a hotel close to everything you'll need for a good family vacation. Charges nightly for parking, though shuttle buses are free. Extra touches such as Mickey Waffles to make the kids feel special.

Hilton Grand Vacations Tuscany Suites on International Drive
Sat Nav Address: 8122 Arrezzo Way, Orlando, 32821
Tel: 407-465-2600
www3.hilton.com/en/hotels/florida/hilton-grand-vacations-tuscany-suites-on-international-drive-ORLINGV/index.html
Location: Adjacent to Premium Outlet Mall

This hotel is convenient for outlet shopping and everything available on tourist-oriented International Drive. All suites come with some sort of a kitchen, depending on choice of room, so it's a good money saver too.

WorldQuest Orlando Resort
Sat Nav Address: 8849 Worldquest Blvd., Orlando, 32821
Tel: 407-387-3800
www.WorldQuestOrlando.com
Location: One mile from Disney World

Every room in this resort is a well-appointed villa with separate sleeping area as well as a full kitchen and handy washer-dryer. Close to Disney but reasonably priced. Free parking, though daily maid service extra charge. Large pool and hot tub area open day and night.

Hilton Orlando
Sat Nav Address: 6001 Destination Parkway, Orlando, 32819
Tel: 407-313-4300
www3.hilton.com/en/hotels/florida/hilton-orlando-
ORLOCHH/index.html
Location: Close to International Drive

Comfortable, allergy-friendly rooms. Massive pool area with lazy river and winding water slide. Seven eateries to dine in. This is a hotel that feels like a resort.

DoubleTree by Hilton
Sat Nav Address: 2305 Hotel Plaza, Lake Buena Vista, 32830
Tel: 407-934-1000
http://doubletree3.hilton.com/en/hotels/florida/doubletree-suites-by-hilton-
hotel-orlando-lake-buena-vista-MCOFHDT/index.html
Location: Disney Springs, Lake Buena Vista

An all-suite hotel with pool and tennis courts, convenient for all things Disney. Each spacious suite has two TVs. Great for families wanting to be close to the action or for couples looking to stay close to nightlife. Free warm chocolate chip cookies at check-in are a nice touch.

Rosen Inn at Pointe Orlando
Sat Nav Address: 9000 International Drive, Orlando, 32819
Tel: 407-996-8585, Toll Free US: 800-999-8585
www.RosenInn9000.com
Location: On I-drive, close to SeaWorld and Pointe Orlando Shops

Handy for all amenities on International Drive and across the road from Point Orlando where there are shops and restaurants and a cinema, this popular large hotel has three pools, 24-hour front desk, and in-room refrigerators and microwaves. Shuttle buses free to Universal but extra charge for Disney. Complimentary transport to Rosen Shingle Creek Golf Club. Nice bonus: At time of writing, children under nine eat free at the buffet restaurant.

$ BUDGET (BELOW $100 PER ROOM, PER NIGHT)

Hampton Inn Orlando – Florida Mall
Sat Nav Address: 8601 S. Orange Blossom Trail, Orlando, 32809
Tel: 407-859-4100, www.HamptonInn.com
Location: Near Florida Mall and Universal Studios

This AAA Three Diamond Approved hotel is within walking distance of Florida Mall (see Florida Mall in SHOPPING TIPS chapter on page 78), though you'll probably need to hire [rent] a car for visiting theme parks. Children stay free under 18. Breakfast buffet included in room rate. **Note:** The Hampton Inn Orlando – Lake Buena Vista is another budget option, close to Disney World.

Clarion Inn & Suites
Sat Nav Address: 5827 Caravan Court, Orlando, 32819
Tel: 407-351-380, www.choicehotels.com
Location: Close to Universal Studios

Clean hotel with comfortable beds, free continental breakfast and an Indian restaurant on-site. Great for walking distance to Universal Studios and Islands of Adventure. Heated pool. No lift [elevator] so you may need the ground floor [first floor] if you have a pushchair [stroller] or don't like or can't manage stairs.

Fairfield Inn, Orlando, Lake Buena Vista in the Marriott Village
Sat Nav Address: 8615 Vineland Avenue, Orlando, 32821
UK Tel: 00800-1927-1927, US Tel: 407-938-9001
www.marriott.com/hotels/travel/mcolz-fairfield-inn-and-suites-orlando-lake-buena-vista-in-the-marriott-village
Location: Lake Buena Vista

Good value hotel with nice-sized pool, close to Disney World and Disney Springs (formerly Downtown Disney). Continental breakfast buffet included in room rate.

TIP Please do extra research when going budget, to be sure you receive the best possible value for money without compromising your holiday.

HOTEL TERMS & TRANSLATIONS

BRITISH	AMERICAN
Bath	Bathtub
Bed Settee	Sofa Bed/Rollaway
Carpet (not fitted)	Rug
Cot	Crib
Curtains	Drapes
Duvet/Eiderdown	Comforter/Quilt
Flannel	Facecloth/Washcloth
Folding Bed	Cot
Full Board	American Plan (AP)
Ground Floor	First Floor
Half Board	Modified American Plan (MAP)
Holiday	Vacation
Lift	Elevator
Loo (as in toilet)	John (slang)
Porter	Bellhop
Toilet	Washroom/Restroom/Bathroom
Reception	Front Desk
Receptionist	Desk Clerk (pronounced clurk)
Settee	Couch
Tap	Faucet
Telly	TV
Wardrobe (Fitted)	Closet

3 HOLIDAY HOME TIPS

Many people prefer to stay in one of the 25,000 holiday homes or studio apartments located in Orlando's tourist hot spots and short-term rental housing estates [sub-divisions]. And why not? Apart from the obvious convenience of cooking facilities, there are many advantages to staying in a holiday home:

- More space and freedom than a hotel room
- Extra privacy
- Family-friendly place to stay
- Your own private pool*
- Extended families and friends often share the cost

*You usually share a communal pool if you're staying in an apartment or townhouse.

But no matter how wonderful, checking into a holiday home can feel a bit like moving house. Stressful at first. Especially arriving following a nine-hour flight, suffering from jet lag, exhausted after a drive on unfamiliar roads. Every house has its own quirks, and Florida homes are somewhat different from British ones, so in this chapter you'll learn what to expect and how to make the most out of your stay.

CHOOSING YOUR HOLIDAY HOME

HANDY HOLIDAY HOME WEBSITES

OwnersDirect.co.uk

HolidayLettings.co.uk

ClickStay.com

VillaDirect.com

FloridaDreamHomes.com

ReunionVacationHomes.com

You'll find dozens of rental agencies and individual owners listed on the Internet; or you'll find homes through travel agencies or via holiday package deals. Try to choose one from a friend's recommendation or a reputable travel company. The closer to Disney – and the bigger the square footage – the higher the price. There's everything from modern studio apartments to 3-bedroom homes with private pools to 8-bedroom, multi-bathroom luxury homes available.

Saving Money: Some families get better rates by staying a few miles out of Orlando, in Polk County in either Davenport or Haines City, for example, and that's fine if you're hiring [renting] a vehicle. It's also cheaper to stay in the shoulder months of spring or autumn [fall] or in the winter season.

CHECKING IN/CHECKING OUT

As mentioned later in the DRIVING TIPS chapter, if your plane lands in the dusk or dark, think seriously about staying overnight at an airport hotel, so you can navigate your way safely to your villa in the light of day. **True Story:** We once arranged for a tow truck to pull a couple's car out of a deep ditch in the dark in the middle of nowhere, because the couple had taken the wrong turn looking for their holiday [vacation] home. They were pretty scared thinking about alligators in the ditch or being stuck overnight on a road without streetlights. The safer option would have been for them to arrange a ride to their villa from the airport, and then pick up locally or have their hire [rental] car delivered the next day.

The Key: Sometimes you'll be asked by the rental company to collect your door key at the main office. Usually, though, there's a key box on the door of the house, and you'll be given a special number code, allowing you to retrieve your key inside the box. At the end of your stay, you must either return the key to the office or leave it in the key box, depending on company policy.

Cleaning Service: Your house or apartment should be spotless when you arrive. If not, let the agency know immediately and they will arrange for a cleaner to arrive. If you require it, later on during your stay, most rental companies will (for an extra charge) provide a mid-stay housekeeping service, where, as well as cleaning the house, the housekeeper will also replace hand and bath towels and change bedding.

Checking-in Time: Your check-in time is usually 4 PM, perhaps earlier if previous guests have left and the property has already been cleaned. If you want to be in the house earlier, or just leave your bags inside, ask if possible. **Checking-out Time:** Is usually 10 AM so that the house can be cleaned for the next guests. Again, ask if you need to extend this. If no other family is booked in after you, you may be in luck.

BABY STUFF

Baby Supplies: When booking, let your agency know you've a baby. Most provide cots [cribs] and highchairs. If you require anything else, such as pushchairs [strollers], check the companies below.

Baby Supply Rentals

BABY'S AWAY
www.BabysAway.com
Tel: 407-334-0232
Delivered to your villa: cots [cribs], pushchairs [strollers], tubs of toys, safety gates, car seats, highchairs, playpens, etc.

KINGDOM STROLLERS
www.KingdomStrollers.com
Tel: 407-674-1866

CHILDREN'S RENTALS
Tel: 407-522-0233

ALL ABOUT KIDS
Tel: 407-812-9300

BRITISH	AMERICAN
Cot	Crib
Dummy	Pacifier
Nappy	Diaper
Pram	Baby Carriage
Pushchair	Stroller
Teat	Nipple

LOCKED OUT!

If you're renting a house with an attached garage, there will be two points of entry:

1. The front door.

2. The garage door. (Inside the garage there is usually a door leading into the house.)

   • The front door will have a deadbolt on it. If you turn this deadbolt to the lock position when you go to bed, and then the next day you exit the house through the garage door, you may be locked out because the garage door, or the door leading to the house, can automatically lock behind you.

   • Now you cannot use your key to open the front door because the deadbolt is in the lock position.

   • For this reason, you (or one of your party) should always use the front door to exit the house. That way, you'll be forced to unlock the deadbolt, saving you a charge from the rental company's locksmith.

 INSIDE THE HOLIDAY HOME

Air Conditioning

The air conditioning will probably be already turned on when you enter the home. The control box and temperature setting is on a wall somewhere, usually in the living room. Find a comfortable setting for your family (probably around 74-76 degrees Fahrenheit in US temperature settings). Don't be heavy-handed with the controls. If you're too hot or too cold, alter by one degree or two at a time.

Important! If you go below 72 degrees you may freeze-up the system. If this happens, turn off for a couple of hours to give the system a chance to defrost. Then wait to gradually bring the temperature back up. If this doesn't work, you'll have to call the rental agency.

- Another reason the air conditioning may not be functioning: the air filter could be dirty (the filter is behind a louvered grate somewhere in the house). The rental agency usually change these monthly, however, if the one in your home is clogged with dust and fluff, wipe clean or call agency for a new one.

- It's also a good idea to go around the house to check all the ceiling air vents are open. Sometimes, other guests close them, and you wonder why the house is not getting any cooler. In some houses, the smaller bedrooms don't get much air, so you may need to keep the doors open at night for extra circulation. Running the ceiling fans also helps the air circulate.

- Keep all entry doors and windows closed or the air conditioning will not operate properly as it will be competing with the outside warm air. It also helps to close the interior blinds when the sun is streaming through.

- To keep costs down, remember to turn air conditioning off while you're out. The house soon cools down, once you turn it back on.

- Occasionally, during the cooler months, you may need to switch the controls over to heating. (Ideal heating temperature is between 65 and 74 degrees.) The weather may heat up again, ensuring the need to switch back to air conditioning, so keep an eye on outside temperature changes.

The Kitchen

Sink and Waste Disposal Unit: There will be two sinks: one for washing, one for rinsing (by the end of your stay, you'll wonder how you ever managed with only one). The sink used for washing may include a waste disposal unit, which you should only operate while running tap water at the same time. You'll find the switch on the wall behind the sink. To avoid breaking the waste disposal unit, don't throw down tealeaves, banana skins, onions, cigarette ends, meat bones or eggshells; and watch out the dishcloth doesn't go down either. Never put your hands down a waste disposal unit if you value your fingers. If something does jam the works, turn the switch off before retrieving. You may then need to press the reset button on the underside of the disposal cylinder (which is usually under the sink) to make it work again.

Dishwasher: Rinse dirty dishes first in the sink with the waste disposal unit. Never pour in washing-up liquid [dish soap] in the dishwasher as it will completely foam-up and a plumber will need to fix it (house owners say this has happened).

Fridge: All homes have lovely big American fridges. It's a good idea to keep leftovers as well as bread and sugar in the fridge to prevent summertime ants and other invading insects.

Cooker [Stove]: The term GRILL is not used: just look for the word BROIL on the temperature controls. Keep the oven door open when grilling [broiling].

Washing Machine: You'll usually find the instructions inside the washing-machine door. American appliances are less complicated than British ones and are easy to operate.

CULTURE SHOCK TIP

Question: Why don't Americans hang washing outside on a line?

Answer: It's seen as unsightly and will lower neighbourhood house prices.

Dryer: As with UK models, the clothes dryer will not work efficiently if lint isn't removed from the dryer's lint screen. If left in the dryer too long, summer clothes such as t-shirts, golf shirts and swimsuits are likely to shrink. Under-dry any clothes you think may shrink, and hang on a hanger in the utility [laundry] room to finish. As Americans don't hang out washing, some homes have a washing line inside the garage just for Brits.

Note: Although any food items must be discarded at the end of your stay, any cleaning provisions can be kindly left in the laundry room for the next guest.

Smoke Detectors: Alarms are often triggered by smoke from cooking. If waving a tea towel [dish towel] underneath the alarm closest to the kitchen does not stop the noise, then switch off by tripping the respective fuse at the fuse box, which is usually situated in the garage. Leave off until smoke dissipates, but don't forget to switch fuse back on.

Refuse [Trash/Garbage]: Always use bin bags [garbage/trash bags]. Collection is probably twice weekly; the days depending on your area (you will probably find days written in the information package left for you). You should place your bins at the bottom of the driveway the night before. Don't put the bins on the street, just on the pavement [sidewalk] or end of the driveway. If you don't drag your bins out, they won't be collected.

Bathrooms

Toilets: Due to small pipes used in American house construction, and different tank systems, toilets block more easily in America than they do in Britain, and are often unable to flush baby wipes, tampons, cotton buds, etc. If a toilet does block, use the plunger provided before calling the rental agency. If this doesn't work, you may be charged for a visit by the plumber.

Taps [faucets]: Unlike the toilets, this time the plumbing is superior to British homes. The shower/bath pipes are always combined hot and cold: turn left for hot water, right for cold. Water often runs piping hot, so help children pour baths and showers.

Bedrooms

Light Switches: You may be forgiven for thinking you're in Australia when you use the light switches, as they work upside down: up for on, down for off. Usually, one of the bedroom lamps is connected to the light switch at the door.

Beds: As mentioned earlier, if you need a baby's cot then request a crib. A bed settee is called a sofa bed or pullout bed or rollaway bed. If you need extra pillows, sheets and blankets, they're usually kept in wardrobes [closets].

TIP Take a moment to check if any radio clock alarms have been set by previous guests. It's not nice being woken at the wrong time.

OUTSIDE THE HOLIDAY HOME

Parking: Fragile plastic irrigation pipes are buried just beneath the garden's [front yard] soil surface, so don't park on the grass or your car could damage them.

Smoking Policies: Most rental agencies operate a no-smoking policy in their homes. Though smoking is allowed outside.

Insects: The pool is screened-in for good reason: to ensure bite-free evenings. Pests include mosquitoes and fire ants. Away from the screened-in area, to prevent bites, you can spray the product 'Off' on your skin, or something with DEET in the ingredients. For a non-chemical product, some people swear by applying 'Skin So Soft' by Avon on their skin. If you do get bitten by mosquitoes, then dab 'After Bite' on your skin to take away the itch. It works like magic, plus it's easy to carry in your bag. And fire ants? They have that name for a reason – their bite burns. Take care not to step or sit on any anthills on the lawn.

Alligators: You may have heard one or two news stories of alligator attacks. Occasionally, you'll hear of alligators sitting in a home's driveway or sitting in a pond overlooking a home. In the unlikely event this happens to you, don't approach the alligator but call the rental agency or the Florida Fish and Wildlife Conservation Commission, Tel: 1-352-732-1225. You'll find more alligator information in WILDLIFE TIPS on page 190.

THE POOL

Most homes come with a private pool and are often the highlight of holidays [vacations], particularly children's. Plus, what better way to cool down after a hot day hitting the theme parks.

Pool Toys: To add to your pool-time enjoyment, you might consider purchasing a couple of pool toys. You can often buy pool toys or lilos [air mattresses] at supermarkets or in stores such as:

PINCH-A-PENNY POOL SUPPLIES (PinchAPenny.com)

WALMART (Walmart.com)

TARGET SUPERSTORES (Target.com)

Beach balls are always fun and inexpensive. It's a good idea to buy one for each child to prevent those it's-my-turn arguments (no they don't always throw to each other as you'd logically think). Floating noodles are great too, and don't cost more than a couple of dollars so you won't mind leaving them behind.

Pool Heat: It's usually an extra fee to heat the pool, though probably worth it, especially outside the hot summer months when the water temperature drops. If there's a pool cover, for safety reasons you must wind back this fully before swimming. Close the cover at night to maintain water temperature.

Pool Alarms: The living room's sliding patio door to the pool is usually fitted with a safety alarm. This emits an ear-splitting noise if someone opens or closes the door without pressing the alarm's button first. Although annoying, this alarm is installed to prevent children from drowning, and it's an offence to try to alter them. To prevent stress, read operating tips below.

How to Operate a Pool Door Alarm

1. Press the alarm button on the wall at the patio door.

2. Open the sliding patio door and step outside.

3. You now have a few seconds to close the door before the alarm goes off.

4. When you step back into the house, press the alarm button again after you've closed the door. If you don't press the alarm button it will make the most horrendous alarm noise.

TIP Make sure any patio door vertical blinds are not twisted or they will stick when you try to open them with the cord.

Do's & Don'ts of Pool Safety and Etiquette

*   Never leave children unattended at the pool. It only takes a couple of minutes for someone to drown. Always have a person in your group keep an eye on children swimming.

*   Never bring glassware to the pool area. If glass breaks, and shards fall into the pool, the whole pool may have to be drained. For this reason always use plastic or paper cups outside.

*   Don't let children run round the pool or they could slip.

*   To prevent being struck by lightning, don't swim during a thunderstorm.

*   Never use the pool for bathing, because soap or shampoo will shut down the filter system.

*   Once a week, the staff from the pool cleaning company will probably show up to clean the pool. Exit the pool while they clean it. If they pour what's called a 'shock' cleaning treatment in, you should keep out of the pool for at least a couple of hours to allow the chemicals to settle.

*   Be considerate and keep the noise down after 9 PM. You are often sharing the estate [sub-division] with full-time house owners who may have to rise early for work.

SHOPPING FOR SUPPLIES

Supermarkets: One of the first things you'll want to do after you arrive is to stock up on food and provisions. The main supermarket chains are either Publix (Publix.com) or Winn-Dixie (WinneDixie.com). Albertsons have now mostly closed.

Superstores: Walmart (Walmart.com) and Target (Target.com) superstores are also popular for grocery shopping, and due to their bulk-purchasing power tend to have some lower-priced items. (By the way: not all Walmart and Target stores sell food.)

Convenience Stores: Usually with higher prices, these include the 7-Eleven (7-Eleven.com) or Circle-K (CircleK.com) chains.

But the closest to an ordinary, everyday supermarket is probably Publix. They also offer local delivery services. Go to website: Publix.com for details or ask your rental agency for the nearest store.

TIP Except when supermarket shopping at Walmart, stand back and enjoy checkout staff pack your groceries for you. No need to tip, even if the staff load your vehicle.

CULTURE SHOCK TIP

'Paper or Plastic?'

Question asked at the cash register [checkout] to see if you'd prefer your groceries packed in paper or plastic bags.

BRITISH PRODUCTS

Many Publix stores offer a selection of British products (found in the 'Ethnic Foods' aisle) and sell, among other items, tea bags, custard, mushy peas and Branston Pickle (all at higher prices due to import costs). To save money and for convenience sake, some people pack in their onboard suitcases their favourite products. Tea bags are the number one item we Brits like to bring, and I must admit American tea is weak in comparison. The stores listed below sell British products, including meat pies, best-back bacon, tea, gifts and real British Cadbury's chocolate*.

THE BRITISH SUPERMARKET
Open 10 AM to 6 PM (closed Sunday)
5695 Vineland Road, Orlando, 32819 (close to Universal Studios)
Tel: 407-370-2023

THE BRITISH SHOPPE
~~809 N. Mills Avenue, Orlando, 32803 (closed Sunday)~~
~~Tel: 407-898-1634~~ 1-321-972-4130
www.TheBritishShoppe.com

TIP Thinking of buying a holiday home in Florida? Go to PROPERTY PURCHASE TIPS on page 155.

HOLIDAY HOME SHOPPING LIST

When the cupboards are bare, grocery shopping feels like you're moving house and starting from scratch, and if you think about it, you are. So on the next page, find a sample list to get you started...

*Regular Cadbury's chocolate products sold in America have added ingredients that change the taste. Despite protests, Hershey's, the American chocolate producers, are trying to ban British chocolate from being imported.

SHOPPING LIST

Bottled Water, Paper Cups (for around the pool)
Bread/Cakes/Biscuits (Cookies)
Cereals
Crackers
Frozen Products (Fish Fingers are called Fish Sticks)
Fruit and Vegetables (in the Produce Aisle)
Ice Cream (Ice-lollies are called Popsicles)
Juice/Pop (Soda)
Ketchup/Mustard/Mayonnaise
Meats and/or Veggie Products
Milk/Eggs/Butter/Cheese/Yogurt/Cream
(Skimmed Milk is 1% or 2% Milk)
Popcorn and Crisps (Chips)
Salad/Salad Dressings (Salad Cream is in the English Section in the
Ethnic Aisle of Publix Supermarket)
Salt/Pepper
Spices and Herbs (pronounced 'Erbs)
Sugar and/or Sweeteners and/or Honey
Sweets (Candies)
Tea/Coffee
Tin Foil (Aluminium [pronounced aloo-minum] Foil)
Barbeque Charcoal + Lighter (if house provides portable barbeque)
Bin Bags (Trash Bags)
Dishwasher Detergent
Fabric Softener or Dryer Sheets
Laundry Detergent/Bleach
Scouring Pads (SOS pads)
Soap/Shower Wash/Shampoo
Toilet Rolls/Tissues/Paper Towels
Toothpaste/Toothbrushes
Washing-up Liquid (Dish Soap)

Note: For a list of stores that sell veggie foods, go to: Health Foods in DINING OUT TIPS chapter on page 93.

TIP To cut down on cooking, many restaurants deliver meals. Check the Yellow Pages, which is probably in a drawer of your rental villa, or search in the House Information binder (if there is one, it's usually left on a coffee table or kitchen bench) for local eateries near you. It's a nice idea to leave the menu that comes with your meal for the next guests to find. The usual tip for restaurant delivery drivers is 15 percent.

GROCERY SHOPPING TERMS & TRANSLATIONS

Because no one in Orlando knows what tinned tomatoes are (Americans say canned), below is a list of grocery shopping terms and translations, which will save you a lot of stress and confusion.

BRITISH	AMERICAN
Aubergine	Eggplant
Beetroot	Beets
Bin Liner	Trash Bag or Garbage Bag
Biscuits	Cookies
Car Park	Parking Lot
Cashpoint/Hole in the Wall	ATM or Cash Machine
Chips	French Fries (or just Fries)
Choc-Ice	Klondike Bar
Clothes Peg	Clothes Pin
Courgettes	Zucchini
Crisps	Chips
Double Cream	Heavy or Whipping Cream
Fish Fingers	Fish Sticks
Gammon	Cured Ham
Greengrocer	Produce Section of Supermarket
Grill	Broil or Grill
Ice-lolly	Popsicle
Jacket Potato	Baked Potato
Jam	Jelly or Jam
Jelly	Jell-O
Joint (of meat)	Roast or Pot Roast

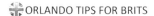

BRITISH	AMERICAN
Lard	Shortening
Lemonade	Fizzy Lemonade/Sprite/7-UP
Liver Sausage	Liverwurst
Lolly or Lollypop	Sucker
Madeira Cake	Pound Cake (similar)
Mineral Water	Bottled or Non-Carbonated Water
Note (as in money)	Bill (as in dollar bill)
Plain Flour	All-purpose Flour
Plaster	Band-Aid
Pop	Soda
Porridge	Oatmeal
Purse	Wallet
Queue	Line-up
Runner Beans	Green Beans
Salad Cream	Mayonnaise or Mayo
Sellotape	Scotch Tape
Serviette	Napkin
Shopping Trolley	Shopping Cart
Skimmed Milk	1% or 2% Milk (or less)
Spring Onion	Green Onion or Scallion
Squash	Concentrated Juice
Still Drinks	Non-carbonated
Stock Cube (OXO)	Bouillon Cube
Sweets	Candy
Swiss Roll	Jelly Roll
Tin (as in tin of soup)	Can
Tin Foil	Aluminium Foil (pronounced Aloo-minum)
Washing-up Liquid	Dish Soap

4 THEME PARK TIPS

The number one reason we Brits travel to Orlando is to experience world-class theme parks. They will certainly live up to your expectations and beyond, but they can also be hot and exhausting, especially if you have young ones in tow. This chapter gives you the scoop on how to make your theme park visit successful and stress free. As well as park descriptions, fun facts and suggested must-do's, you'll discover some all-important ticket buying tips, how to avoid unbearably long queues, and how to keep cool and comfortable in the hot, humid Florida weather.

PLANNING & BOOKING

One of the secrets to an enjoyable park experience is to do some prior planning. With the help of a Disney or Universal website or park map, you can find out what rides you want to go on, shows you want to see, fast passes you want to use, what ride height restrictions are in place, and what restaurants or cafes you may want to dine in. Planning saves you from wandering aimlessly around these massive parks in the heat. And booking in advance avoids the disappointment of turning up to find a tour or restaurant already full.

TIP DISNEY EVENTS/TOURS Tel: 407-WDW-TOUR (939-8687) UK Tel: 0870-242-4900 https://disneyworld.disney.go.com/events-tours and **DISNEY DINING** Tel: 407-WDW-DINE (939-3463) UK Disney Dining Tel: 0800-169-0748 https://disneyworld.disney.go.com/help/dining-reservations can be booked up to 180 days before your trip.

Busiest Times of Year: During the summer months, July and August are the busiest, with the Fourth of July holiday especially crazy. In the so-called winter or off-season, parks close earlier with fewer shows or restaurants open. However, it can be particularly pleasant walking around a huge theme park during the cooler, less crowded months. To help avoid long lines in the heat and humidity see the table below. See also Queue Jumping later in this chapter.

BALANCE IT

To give you and your family much needed time to recoup, alternate your theme park visits with days by the pool, or a trip to the cinema [movie theatre], or you can chill out at one of the quieter places in the OFF THE THEME PARK TRACK chapter on page 133.

Times of Year to Avoid 90-Minute Queues		
Slowest Months	**When Exactly**	**Weather**
January/ February	After New Year but before Spring Break (before March/April period)	Weather is unpredictable – pack jackets, jeans, jumpers [sweaters]
May	Late May to early June but avoid Memorial Day long weekend (last Monday of May)	Usually fine weather. Memorial Day marks the first day of summer for Americans
September	After the Labour Day long weekend (first Monday of September) Note: Halloween Horror Nights at Universal Studios during mid Sept through Oct can be busy	Weather is usually sunny and pleasant with less humidity and less afternoon rain showers. Labour Day marks the last day of summer for Americans
October/ November	Avoid week around Thanksgiving (fourth Thursday in November)	Weather is mild and pleasant making October a popular month for Brits
December	Avoid Christmas week	Same weather as January/February

TIP Children under three are free in all Disney and Universal parks.

Keeping Kids Happy

Want happy children on holiday [vacation]? Then the American Psychiatric Association suggests you . . .

- Bring snacks, books and games while travelling.
- Try to maintain a routine, as children are reassured by predictability.
- Plan plenty of bathroom and snack breaks.
- Don't force kids to tolerate adult activities such as long museum visits or formal dinners.
- Let older ones help plan the trip.

TIP Have breakfast before going to a theme park because most parks don't have many options for this early meal.

 THEME PARK TICKETS

A good idea is to purchase your park tickets on the first day of your holiday [vacation] before money runs out. Alternatively, to save precious time, purchase tickets prior to your arrival. Except for water parks, theme parks are open every day of the year and most types of tickets are good for any day. Another idea is to put aside a set of tickets for the end of your stay, then you'll still have something to look forward to if cash runs low. But, if you can afford to, it's more economical to purchase multi-day, park-hopping tickets. (More details later in this chapter.)

Where to Buy Tickets

1. Inside theme parks.
2. Online at www.DisneyWorld.co.uk and at www.UniversalOrlando.co.uk
3. At UK travel agencies or reputable discount ticket agencies such as:
   - Attraction Tickets Direct: UK Tel: 0845-130-3876 or 0800-086-1699, www.AttractionTicketsDirect.com
   - Undercover Tourist: UK Tel: 0800-081-1702, www.UndercoverTourist.com
   - Floridatix: UK Tel: 0800-980-5552, www.Floridatix.co.uk

4. At Disney stores inside the Orlando International Airport.
5. At some Orlando hotels.
6. At Walmart stores that have travel agencies in them.
7. At the Official Visitor Centre:

OFFICIAL VISITOR CENTER [note American spelling]
8723 International Drive, Suite 101, Orlando, 32819
Tel: 407-363-5872 or
US Toll Free: 1-800-972-3304
www.VisitOrlando.com

Open every day of the year, 8:30 AM to 6:30 PM, except Christmas Day. For maps, apps, calendar of events, tourist and family reunion advice, information on hotels, attractions and discounted tickets.

THEME PARK RULES

You can bring snacks and water but don't bring packed picnics to theme parks. For other rules, go to . . .
DISNEY theme-park rules:
https://disneyworld.disney.go.com/park-rules
UNIVERSAL theme-park rules:
www.universalorlando.com/Resort-Information/Policies-and-Restrictions.aspx

Nuisance Warning: Throughout Central Florida you will spot tourist information booths. There are two types: Those that sell theme-park tickets as well as provide general tourist information, and those that have agents who pounce on you to try and persuade you to tour their time-share properties, offering free theme-park tickets as incentive (they are even inside some Orlando hotels). These time-share sales meetings will take up a big chunk of your precious time and really give you the hard sell. So, unless you are seriously in the market for a time-share apartment, it's not worth it.

TIP Avoid ticket booths on the side of the road because they could be selling out-of-date or fraudulent tickets.

DISNEY TICKETS

https://disneyworld.disney.go.com/en_GB

Disney tickets are from one-day entrance to ten days (or annual passes) also the Ultimate Ticket 7-14 days (below). You can also purchase add-ons for different options, such as Park Hopper add-on or Water Park add-on.

Disney Park Hopper: Tickets include Disney's four theme parks: Magic Kingdom, Hollywood Studios, EPCOT, and Animal Kingdom.

Disney Ultimate Ticket: Exclusively designed for UK visitors (7 or 14 days), tickets cover the four Disney parks, plus two water parks, ESPN Wide World of Sports, and DisneyQuest Indoor Interactive Theme Park. However, these tickets cannot be purchased in Florida (you can buy from UK travel agents or ticket agents noted on WHERE TO BUY TICKETS above). They expire after 14 days, whether you've used the days up or not.

UNIVERSAL TICKETS

www.UniversalOrlando.co.uk

(Make sure you type co.uk and not .com to get to the UK site)

Universal offer either one day or multi-day tickets (or annual passes), as well as park hopping to Islands of Adventure – all at special prices for Brits.

The Flex Ticket: At time of writing, one of the most popular tickets for Brits is the 14-day, 5-park (Universal Studios, Islands of Adventure, Wet 'n Wild (closing permanently December 2016), Aquatica, SeaWorld) unlimited access Flex Ticket – good for entrance at any time parks are open.

The Flex Ticket Plus: Covers everything the Flex Ticket above offers, plus transport and entry to Busch Gardens theme park in Tampa Bay (BuschGardens.com).

TIP Universal Flex tickets expire after 14 consecutive days.

PARKING TIPS

TIP Take a digital photo of your parking location (e.g. Goofy area, spot number 234) so at the end of a long day you can find your vehicle. If you haven't got a camera, just scribble a note of your spot and keep it safe.

Other Parking Tips:

- Car Parks [parking lots] at theme parks charge $17 per day for a car or bike, more for other vehicles like a camper van [RV].
  You pay only once a day no matter how many parks visited.
  Important! Keep receipt to show to next park.

- Parking is FREE for Disney or Universal hotel guests (show proof), as well as select annual pass holders. Disney water park parking is also free, and so is ESPN World of Sports, as well as Disney Springs (formerly Downtown Disney).

- Parking charges are reduced after 6 PM (sometimes you are just waved through).

- When you've parked your car at a Disney theme park, catch a tram (ferry or tram at Magic Kingdom) to take you inside the park. Don't worry, you won't have to wait long. However, when it's crazy busy, avoid Magic Kingdom's big ferry if you suffer from claustrophobia.

TIP The Universal Studios Parking Garage Address is at: 6000 Universal Boulevard, Orlando, 32819. Universal also offer valet-parking services.

The American Adventure, EPCOT

MOBILITY – PUSHCHAIR & WHEELCHAIR RENTAL

Pushchairs [strollers]: Single and double pushchair [stroller] rentals are available at the park entrances on a first come, first served basis, and toddlers and small children enjoy being pushed around these huge parks in them, saving strain on their little legs. Also consider using a pushchair [stroller] even if your child is no longer using one at home, because the extra heat can be exhausting for older tots too.

TIP Keep your theme park pushchair or wheelchair receipt if you wish to go to more than one park in a day, and you won't have to pay again.

For Pushchair Rental Delivered to Your US Home or Hotel:

BABY'S AWAY
Tel: 407-334-0232
www.BabysAway.com

KINGDOM STROLLERS
Tel: 407-674-1866
www.KingdomStrollers.com

WALKER MOBILITY
US Toll Free: 1-888-726-6837
Tel. 407-518-6000
www.WalkerMobility.com

Wheelchairs: For the disabled, easy to operate electric and non-electric wheelchairs and electric convenience vehicles (also called scooters) are available just inside park entrances. Again, on a first come, first served basis. You can also pick up here the DAS (Disability Access Service) card for front of line access.

For Wheelchair Rental Delivered to Your US Home or Hotel:

SCOOT AROUND
US Toll Free: 1-888-441-7575
www.ScootAround.com

WALKER MOBILITY
Tel. 407-518-6000
US Toll Free: 1-888-726-6837
www.WalkerMobility.com

QUEUE JUMPING

To cut down on long queues, Disney has the free FASTPASS+, and Universal Studios and Islands of Adventure have the EXPRESS PLUS ticket (not free) – especially useful during the busy summer months because these tickets gain you access to fast-track queues [line-ups].

TIP Keep a sharp eye on multiple queues for rides and shows. Sometimes no one is lining-up at one for no other reason than people in a crowd tend to follow each other like sheep. We've often just walked up to an empty or short queue because no one else thinks it's a way in.

Disney FASTPASS+: At certain rides and shows, each member of your party can choose a FASTPASS+ time slot. There is no charge. Here are the rules at time of writing . . .

1. Insert your entrance ticket in the FASTPASS+ kiosk machine.

2. Select the rides you want. Three per day, initially. Then you can add one more at a time (after you've used the first three).

3. You don't get a ticket anymore, so make a note of the times to the ride or experience.

4. You'll have an arrival window time of about an hour, so you don't have to rush for the exact time.

5. Go to the ride and tap your entrance ticket on the tap post.

6. At time of writing, if you miss your allotted time, no worries, you can book another.

Important! You have to guess which rides will be busy, so it's best to pick up FASTPASS+ slots for major rides or shows, and pick them up early.

TIP FASTPASS+ App. You can reserve online your access ahead of time with the My Disney Experience app:
https://disneyworld.disney.go.com/plan/my-disney-experience/mobile-apps

Disney MYMAGIC+: Disney hotel guests and annual passholders wear the MagicBand wristband to use for their room key, park tickets, FASTPASS+ and reservations.

Note: Disney hotel guests can reserve rides 60 days in advance and then (at the theme parks) use their MagicBand at the tap post. Everyone else can reserve 30 days in advance. For more details, go to website:
https://disneyworld.disney.go.com/plan/my-disney-experience/bands-cards

Apple Watch (www.Apple.com/watch): Disney have partnered with Apple so you can use the Apple Watch for Disney purchases with a single-step payment. Cashiers can't see your card number, name or security code, making it safe to use. There's even a Mickey character you can choose for the watch face.

TIP Don't ever illegally jump into an EXPRESS PASS or FASTPASS+ queue. The staff check more than once if you're allowed to be there.

Disney: Free Water Taxi Transportation Points

MAGIC KINGDOM by boat from:
• Grand Floridian Resort & Spa
• Polynesian Village Resort
• Fort Wilderness Resort and Campground
• Wilderness Lodge
• Polynesian Villas & Bungalows

EPCOT and **HOLLYWOOD STUDIOS** by boat from:
• Boardwalk Inn and Villas Resort
• Beach Club Resort
• Yacht Club Resort
• Walt Disney World Swan Hotel
• Walt Disney World Dolphin Hotel

DISNEY SPRINGS area by boat from:
• Port Orleans Resort
• Old Key West Resort
• Saratoga Springs Resort

Universal EXPRESS PASS: For Universal Studios or Islands of Adventure – this pass buys you one time access to popular rides or shows on lines that promise to be super fast. A day costs anywhere from $19.99 up to $140 per person! Depending on time of year or whether you want an EXPRESS PASS ticket for one park or two.

- There's no time slot allocated, you just line-up in the EXPRESS PASS line, which won't take you to the front of the queue but you'll be in a much shorter line than the regular one, depending on time of day. Sometimes you'll shave an hour or more off your wait time to popular rides in the middle of the day. Sometimes 30 minutes or less.

- A limited number of these tickets go on sale at either Universal Studios or Islands of Adventure, one hour after opening. You can also buy them online at UniversalOrlando.com.

Unlimited EXPRESS PASS: You can also bundle your Universal theme park admittance ticket with this pass, allowing you to use the express lanes as many time as you want. It may even cost you less to do this than buying all your tickets separately.

Are Universal EXPRESS PASSES Worth It? Check the list of attractions the Universal EXPRESS PASS covers, as this extra cost is only worth it if you're going to use most of the rides on the list. Unlike the Disney FASTPASS, you won't be tied to a time slot. But then again, the Disney system is free. It's also not worth buying if the rides you want don't have long wait times anyway. And, if you're here mainly for The Wizarding World of Harry Potter, then don't bother (see **Important!** note next page).

FIREWORKS, SHOWS & PARADES*!*

Find your watching spot a half hour beforehand – or earlier if you see people grabbing prime spots – to get a jump on the view-blocking crowd.

Staying at a Universal Resort: If you're staying at one of the three Universal properties: Royal Pacific Resort, Hard Rock Hotel or Portofino Bay Hotel (not Cabana Bay Beach), then you can receive an UNLIMITED EXPRESS PASS included in your stay. You use the fast lines as many times as you like, so that's a wonderful bonus and can even ensure it's worth staying at these luxury hotels if you're going to buy the passes anyway. In other words, it could cost you the same as staying at a budget hotel with the ticket savings you make.

Important! At time of writing, the EXPRESS PASS does NOT cover the Harry Potter rides: Escape to Gringots, Harry Potter and the Forbidden Journey, or the Hogwarts Express steam train.

Note: Unless you're purchasing a 2-park EXPRESS PASS, you have to pay for an Islands of Adventure pass separately.

KEEPING COOL AND COMFORTABLE

Summer heat and humidity can drain your energy, make your children whine, give you a headache, and generally spoil your fun. Because theme parks are suntraps, the temperature feels higher than everywhere else in Orlando. I call it the T.P.T. or Theme Park Temperature factor. I add 5-10 degrees to the day's weather forecast to allow for the T.P.T. factor. To help you keep cool in the blistering sun, check out the following...

Preventing Meltdown: Nothing beats that feeling of excitement when you first enter an Orlando theme park, so don't ruin your day by overdoing it. Perhaps you've saved all year for this holiday [vacation] and don't want to miss a thing. It's better, though, to enjoy half the park at a slower speed than rush around wearing yourself out, not really enjoying everything you do. Remember, it's the quality of the trip that's important, not how much you can get crammed in. And because little ones get exhausted quickly in the heat, allow for plenty of breaks and refreshments. Then everyone will go home with good memories.

The Early Bird: Go to popular rides early in the morning before they develop long lines (or late in the day when everyone else is watching the fireworks and parades). Make use of the free Disney FASTPASS+ or if you can afford to, the Universal EXPRESS PASS (see Queue Jumping, page 47).

Take Breaks: During the mid-day sun, perhaps splurge on a sit-down, air-conditioned lunch and take time to cool down, rest and refuel. Or at any time, you may leave the park, receiving a stamp on your hand at the exit gate so you can return later to enjoy the rides and end-of-day shows when the temperature has dropped.

Important! To re-enter a park, either use your MagicBand (and fingerprint) or entrance ticket.

Late for a Change: If you've purchased a multi-day, park-hopper ticket (or annual pass), and don't feel like spending a full day in the blistering heat. Or perhaps you're exhausted from previous theme-park days. Why not try going later in the day. Set off to time your arrival inside a park for late afternoon when the summer sun is less intense. Plus, in the summer, it's still warm after dark and you'll have roughly five hours park time left (check park closing times first.)

Note: In the interests of animal welfare, 6-8 PM is closing time at Disney's Animal Kingdom.

Clothing: On hot, sticky days wear cool cotton tees or shirts and shorts or capris. A few teens even change into a bikini top and shorts for water rides that soak (rain ponchos sold in parks or supermarkets keep you dry too). For children, have them wear bright clothing that's easy to spot. Let them get wet by running into interactive fountains or take them on log flumes or other rides that splash. For this reason, many parents have their children wear a swimsuit underneath clothing they can quickly whip off.

TIP No matter how hot it is, men you must keep your shirt on inside theme parks or you'll be asked politely to put it back on.

Footwear: You'll be walking miles, so comfortable shoes are a must – trainers [sneakers] are your best bet. Now is not the time to break in those new shoes or sandals.

MISTING STATIONS
Cool your body under theme park outside air conditioners that spray fine mists of refreshing water.

Fans: Perhaps invest in one of those battery-operated, portable fans that spray water – a good way to keep cool in long queues [lines]. You can buy them at parks, or beforehand in supermarkets and pharmacies, as well as at some gift stores.

Shade: For protection from the glaring sun, wear sunglasses and throw on a sun hat or baseball cap. A sun hat is important for babies, too, and many Brits – unaccustomed to such strong sunshine – often forget them.

Hydration and Headaches: Drink plenty of water to prevent sunstroke, avoiding a visit to the A&E [Emergency Department or ER]. And, if you're hooked on tea and tend to get a headache without a cup, take along your headache pills because you're not going to easily find a cup of tea at theme parks (except maybe at the English pub at EPCOT), although you will find other caffeine-laden drinks such as coffee and cola. Also, take along your headache pills if you're prone to heat-induced headaches.

TIP A veteran Disney employee told us: 'To avoid headaches in the heat, wear a sun hat, drink lots of water and – what people often forget – eat something. Lack of food can cause a headache.'

China, EPCOT

THEME PARK ENTRANCES

Take a pause inside the park entrance to look over your theme-park map and, if you haven't already done so, plan your day. Here you'll find notices of times of shows and parades. You'll also find services, such as foreign currency exchange, dining reservations, pushchair [stroller] and wheelchair rentals, lockers, first-aid, and lost and found.

Lost and Found: Theme-park visitors lose roughly 1000 personal items per day – including false teeth and prosthetic limbs! – which, if unclaimed, eventually get sold at staff yard sales or donated to charity. (For lost and found contact phone numbers, go to: HANDY PHONE NUMBERS at the back of this book).

Intense Rides: Use common sense when choosing rides, especially if you have any medical conditions such as heart disorders or neck and back problems. Pregnant women should be particularly careful. Though it's a good idea for anyone, not just those with medical conditions, to take breaks in-between intense rides.

TIP Search YouTube.com to watch actual theme park rides in action – a good way to tell if a ride is suitable for every person in your group.

Children on Rides: Some rides are only suitable for older children or adults, and it's unadvisable to let very young ones on these extreme rides. Never put a child on a ride when he or she is crying or upset. Your child's personality will determine what she or he can and cannot handle. Check park maps for warnings, or ask for advice at Guest Services at the park entrances; the staff there will let you know which rides are in the dark or extra scary. But if after boarding a ride your child becomes upset, before the ride starts let an attendant know, so that she can let you both off.

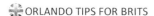

HOW HIGH?

To avoid disappointment, check children's ride height restrictions before you visit a theme park. Either online or on your park map.

Disney Height Requirements:

https://disneyworld.disney.go.com/attractions

Universal Height Requirements:

www.universalorlando.com/Resort-Information/Ride-Height-Requirements.aspx

CHILD SWAP/RIDER SWITCH SERVICE

If a ride is not suitable for a child in your party, you can take advantage of the CHILD SWAP service (also known as RIDER SWITCH) at either Disney or Universal parks. This way, the members in your party can take turns going on a ride while someone in your group looks after your infant or child. Plus ...

- If there are only three members of your party, one person is allowed to enjoy the ride twice, so no one has to ride alone.

- When you arrive at a ride, be sure to let the attendant (or Disney 'cast member') know you want to use the swap service. They will show you the procedure for that ride and you can take turns without the other adults in the party having to queue again.

TIP Disney gives you a Child Swap ticket, so you can go off with your young one and do other things. At Universal you have to wait at the ride.

Meet and Greet Mickey

Ride Safety Tips

- Read park warnings to determine if a ride is suitable for all the members in your party.
- Never attempt to cheat height restrictions. They are there for your child's personal safety.
- Don't ride if you're feeling unwell or under the influence of alcohol or drugs. Make sure your health can manage extreme rides (such as heart conditions, pregnancy, asthma attacks).
- Before setting off on a ride, make sure the lap bar or seat belt is securely in place.
- At all times keep hands, feet and hair inside ride. Don't ever stand.
- Prevent missiles by ensuring personal items such as coins, phones, sunglasses, cameras and other loose items can't fall from your pockets and bags.
- Just before a ride finishes, lean forward slightly to save your back being bumped by a sudden stop.

THEME PARK ENTERTAINMENT DISTRICTS

Before we get to the individual theme parks, below are three places you can go to for entertainment, dining and shopping or simply sightseeing and people watching. Free to enter, two are owned by Disney, and one by Universal.

TIP Bars and Clubs usually have a small cover charge after 9 PM.

UNIVERSAL CITYWALK *Sat Nav Address: 6000 Universal Boulevard, Orlando, 32819. Tel: 407-224-2690. Location: Off I-4 East, Exit 75A. www.CityWalkOrlando.com*

Universal CityWalk is an entertainment district popular for nightlife and dining, and includes a meandering boardwalk next to a lake with eateries, shops and stalls. There's also the huge Universal Cineplex for films [movies], and for restaurants you'll find: Hard Rock Cafe, The Bubba Gump Shrimp Co., Red Oven Pizza Bakery, and Antojito's Authentic Mexican Food, to name a few. (More next page)

CityWalk nightclub and pub scene have venues such as the multi-level tropical Red Coconut Club, the Rising Star, where you can perform karaoke to a live band Tuesday-Saturday, the Mardi Gras themed Pat O'Brien's, and Bob Marley open-air gazebo for live Reggae and food.

A major live show, at time of writing, is the unique Blue Man Group (www.universalorlando.com/Shows/Blue-Man-Group.aspx).

CityWalk also have an array of one-of-a-kind stores (for more information, go to: Theme Park Shopping Districts in SHOPPING TIPS chapter on page 82).

DISNEY SPRINGS (formerly Downtown Disney) *Sat Nav Address: 1494 E. Buena Vista Drive, Lake Buena Vista, 32830. Tel: 407-WDW-MAGIC (939-6244) Location: Off I-4 or off Highway 192 https://disneyworld.disney.go.com/destinations/disney-springs*

Disney Springs has undergone a major refurbishment, which has doubled its size since being Downtown Disney. You'll find restaurants, shops and entertainment in an area divided into four main sections: The Town Centre, Marketplace, West Side, and The Landing.

Note: The nightclub mecca called Pleasure Island is no more.

Here's a taste of what's currently on offer...

- Cirque du Soleil (CirqueDuSoleil.com): a theatre with live shows.
- AMC Pleasure Island 24: a 24-screen cinema.
- DisneyQuest: an indoor interactive theme park.
- Characters in Flight: a tethered balloon flight rising to 400 feet.
- House of Blues (HouseOfBlues.com): a club and restaurant.
- Planet Hollywood (PlanetHollywood.com): a themed restaurant.
- A mix of specialty shops and restaurants, including a Harley-Davidson store, Raglan Road Irish Pub & Bar, Fuego by Sosa Cigars, and the Paradiso 37 waterfront restaurant.

EARL OF SANDWICH
www.EarlofSandwichUSA.com

The British 11th EARL OF SANDWICH – a direct descendant of the inventor of the sandwich – is the owner of the Earl of Sandwich cafe at Disney Springs Marketplace.

Coincidentally, his American partner is named Robert EARL.

The Earl's son had the idea and his name is ORLANDO*!*

DISNEY HOTELS CLOSE TO DISNEY SPRINGS
Disney's Port Orleans Resort French Quarter
Disney's Port Orleans Resort – Riverside
Disney's Saratoga Springs Resort & Spa
Disney's Old Key West Resort

DISNEY'S BOARDWALK *Sat Nav Address: 2101 N. Epcot Resorts Blvd, Lake Buena Vista, 32830*
https://disneyworld.disney.go.com/destinations/boardwalk
Location: Near EPCOT

Disney's Boardwalk is designed to be reminiscent of an old American seaside town, with gentle activities that include boating on the lake and fringe-top surrey bike rentals. The boardwalk is a pleasant place for strolling around shops and restaurants or just watching a lakeside sunset while enjoying an ice cream.

DISNEY HOTELS CLOSE TO DISNEY'S BOARDWALK
Disney's BoardWalk Inn
Disney's Boardwalk Villas

TIP For advice from an expert panel of mums [moms] on all things Disney, ask the Moms' Panel at: http://DisneyParksMomsPanel.disney.go.com

THEME PARKS

In this section, you'll find the descriptions and backgrounds of each major Orlando theme park, along with fun facts, highlights and helpful tips.

DISNEY'S MAGIC KINGDOM *Sat Nav Address: 3111 World Drive, Lake Buena Vista, 32830. Tel: 407-824-4321 Location: Walt Disney World. Off I-4, Exit 64 www.Disneyworld.com or www.Disneyworld.co.uk*

Magic Kingdom is divided into six lands . . .

Main Street

Adventureland

Frontierland

Liberty Square

(New) Fantasyland

Tomorrowland

Magic Kingdom for Young Ones: With theme parks catering more and more to thrill-seeking teens, it's nice for families here that rides at Magic Kingdom are often suitable for small children, especially Peter Pan's Flight, The Many Adventures of Winnie the Pooh, The Magic Carpets of Aladdin. Cinderella's Golden Carrousel, Mad Tea Party, Dumbo the Flying Elephant, and It's a Small World. Recently renovated New Fantasyland features Under the Sea – Journey of the Little Mermaid, Ariel's Grotto, the new Seven Dwarfs Mine Train, and Enchanted Tales with Bella.

TIP Tomorrowland Terrace is a wonderful terrace cafe overlooking Cinderella Castle where you can watch Disney's Magic Kingdom fireworks and enjoy a yummy dessert. Tel: 407-WDW-DINE (939-3463) or UK Tel: 0800-169-0748. https://disneyworld.disney.go.com/dining/magic-kingdom/tomorrowland-terrace-fireworks-dessert-party

In his life, Walt Disney valued most the family unit and these two things: nostalgia and technology, and he blended these to create wonderful movies and Magic Kingdom, a place for all the family to enjoy.

Magic Kingdom Highlights

Space Mountain: An indoor rollercoaster at high speeds in the dark.

Seven Dwarfs Mine Train: A ride through Snow White's countryside, then into the diamond mine.

Splash Mountain: A log flume that drops five stories.

Wishes: Spectacular end-of-day fireworks show.

DISNEY'S EPCOT *Sat Nav Address: 1200 Epcot Resort Blvd., Lake Buena Vista, 32830. Tel: 407-824-4321. Location: Walt Disney World, off I-4, Exit 67. www.Disneyworld.com or www.Disneyworld.co.uk*

EPCOT originally stood for Experimental Prototype Community of Tomorrow – a futuristic city planned by Walt Disney where people could actually live, work and play. But after Walt died, the company vetoed the original design and EPCOT instead became a round-the-world showcase theme park, one of Orlando's most relaxing parks to visit, filled with international restaurants and mostly mild rides. The biggest Orlando theme park, it can take more than one day to discover, so wear comfortable shoes and perhaps take advantage of the free ferry in the central lagoon.

EPCOT is divided into two parts...

- FUTURE WORLD: Filled with rides and scientific exhibits celebrating the Universe (see below).

- WORLD SHOWCASE: Filled with eleven different nations, showcasing each country's architecture and restaurants, with a few rides interspersed throughout, and stores that sell international products.

Epcot's World Showcase Countries

Canada

China

France

Germany

Italy

Japan

Mexico

Morocco

Norway

United Kingdom

United States

EPCOT Events: During April-June the **Flower and Garden Festival** is in full bloom, with extra displays of flowers and topiary sculptures often shaped into Disney characters, as well as gardening exhibits and lectures.

FROZEN ALERT

Norway in EPCOT's World Showcase will feature, from the phenomenally successful movie *Frozen*, a **Frozen Ever After** ride by the summer of 2016.

In the autumn [fall] EPCOT hosts (for two or three weeks) the popular **International Food and Wine Festival,** presenting special exhibits, seminars, demonstrations, as well as food and wine and beer tasting from over twenty different countries. Small, sample plates of food are on sale, and in the past, these have included dishes like Guinness Stew, Escargot Provençale and Vegetarian Curry.

Epcot's Future World

The other section of EPCOT – Future World – is all about discovering the incredible world we live in and learning to appreciate it. Here you'll find the majority of EPCOT'S rides. By the way, the noise coming from the **Test Track** car-racing ride sounds a lot scarier than the ride actually is.

On the other hand, **Mission: Space** – a 100 million dollar space flight-simulator that took five years and 650 people to plan and build – is an intense ride unsuitable for young children or anyone claustrophobic, or anyone who even suspects they have a medical condition such as high blood pressure or a heart problem. (Though, you can now choose the milder version of this ride, which is minus the ride's spinning centrifuge).

But by far one of the most relaxing yet inspiring rides at Future World is **Soarin'** (see Highlights below). After riding Soarin', people often give it a round of applause!

TIP You can book your Disney advanced dining reservation to coincide with EPCOT'S nightly fireworks show. Tel: 407-WDW-DINE (939-3463) or UK Tel: 0800-169-0748 https://disneyworld.disney.go.com. For the best views, dine in: 'England' at the Rose and Crown Pub terrace, or 'Mexico' at the outdoor dining section of Cantina de San Angel restaurant, or 'Morocco' at the outdoor dining at Spice Road Table.

EPCOT Highlights

The Seas with Nemo and Friends: Great for little ones, this 'undersea' clam ride is based on the movie *Finding Nemo*.

Mission: Space (see description above).

Soarin': Simulated smooth hang-gliding ride over the Californian coastal and vineyard regions.

IllumiNations: Fireworks and laser light show.

Much of Walt Disney's early inspiration comes from his European travels to England, Germany, France and Italy, and the buildings and architecture he saw there and the books he read, such as: Aesop's Fables, The Jungle Book, Adventures of Pinocchio, Sleeping Beauty and Cinderella. You can see all these influences as you stroll around his wonderful theme parks.

DISNEY'S HOLLYWOOD STUDIOS *Sat Nav Address: 351 South Studio Drive, Lake Buena Vista, 32830. Tel: 407-824-4321. Location: Walt Disney World, off I-4, Exit 64 www.DisneyWorld.com or www.DisneyWorld.co.uk*

Hollywood Studios (formerly MGM-Studios) is a working movie and TV studios complete with soundstages and backlots. All the rides, shows and play areas are movie- and television-based, including Toy Story Mania!, The Great Movie Ride, Honey, I Shrunk the Kids playground, and the stomach-dropping Twilight Zone Tower of Terror.

Shows: Check the Tip Board just inside park entrance, for times and locations of shows at Hollywood Studios. Note: Some shows are closed in the evening.

TIP New Year's Eve party at Hollywood Studios is popular with locals and visitors alike, however, teens may prefer Universal's CityWalk's New Year's Eve party. Best to arrive early at either event, before parks fill to capacity.

Hollywood Studios Highlights

Beauty and the Beast Live on Stage: Colourful live show popular with girls.

Indiana Jones Epic Stunt Spectacular: Live show based on the iconic movie: *Raiders of the Lost Ark.*

Fantasmic!: After-dark presentation, featuring Mickey, dancing water and laser/fireworks displays.

Lights, Motors, Action!: Hair-raising car stunt show for lovers of car chase movies.

Toy Story Mania!: A 3-D ride and video shooting game. Fun Fact: Mr Potato Head took longer to programme than any other Disney animatronic.

DISNEY'S ANIMAL KINGDOM *Sat Nav Address:*
Osceola Parkway, Lake Buena Vista, 32830. Tel: 407-824-4321
Location: Walt Disney World, off I-4, Exit 65. www.Disneyworld.com or www.Disneyworld.co.uk

As the folks at Disney will tell you, Animal Kingdom is not a zoo and does not remotely resemble one. Set on five hundred lush acres, this innovative park has 1700 animals and over 20 attractions and rides.

TIP The best time to see the animals at Animal Kingdom is in the cool of the morning at feeding time, or just before closing, around 5 or 6 PM. That's when you'll see the powerful silverback gorillas being coaxed with food back into their sleeping enclosure.

RESCUE PLAN

Animal Kingdom is a member of the
American Zoo and Aquarium Association
Species Survival Plan: www.aza.org

Kilimanjaro Safari: For a tour alongside hippo-filled rivers and elevated Savannah (tropical flat grassland) try this popular safari. African animals roam freely, and each safari vehicle is environmentally friendly, fuelled by liquid propane for cleaner air.

Pangani Forest Trail: A walking tour to see animals, not in cages but roaming the land, many protected from visitors by moats.

TIP Disney's Animal Kingdom Lodge is the hotel attached to this park. It has the most amazing vaulted African ceiling on the ground floor, so be sure to check it out. To gain the full Animal Kingdom experience, you can stay at the lodge and witness giraffes feeding right outside your balcony (certain rooms only).

Animal Kingdom Highlights

Kali River Rapids: Popular winding water raft ride where you'll get wet, possibly soaked. Great for a hot day.

The Tree of Life: Has 325 animal carvings on the tree. There's even a show to watch inside.

Expedition Everest – Legend of the Forbidden Mountain: A thrilling train adventure that takes you up a 200-foot mountain and down 80-foot drops, sometimes backwards. Lurking in the shadows is the abominable snowman. For inspiration, Disney imagineers visited the Eastern Himalayas.

Note: An exciting $500 million-dollar new Avatar Land is planned for Animal Kingdom (2017 opening), based on the creative Avatar movies by James Cameron.

UNIVERSAL STUDIOS *Parking Garage: 6000 Universal Boulevard, Orlando, 32819. Location: Off the I-4 (after parking your vehicle at Universal's Parking Garage, walk to the end of CityWalk, and it's on the right) Tel: 407-363-8000 (General Number) Tel: 407-224-4233 (Guest Services) www.UniversalOrlando.com*

Universal Studios' multi-million dollar, state-of-the-art rides all have a Hollywood theme. Just walking around here makes you feel part of the cinema. Look up, and you're in the middle of New York's high-rise buildings; turn right, and you're suddenly on a London street. Everywhere you go, the attention to detail is astounding; not surprising considering Steven Spielberg is a creative consultant to Universal.

TIP Universal Studios and Islands of Adventure are situated next to each other, within walking distance (at the end of Universal CityWalk).

Mardi Gras at Universal Studios: Universal Mardi Gras carnival is held Saturday nights during the spring. Features floats, stilt walkers, costumed characters, live music and Cajun and Creole cuisine.

Universal Studios Highlights

Diagon Alley: Inspired from the Harry Potter films and books, Diagon Alley, complete with shops, eateries and Escape from Gringots ride (includes plunging and spinning elements and riders must be at least 42" tall).

Hogwart's Express Train: At Universal Studios you can catch the Hogwart's Express steam train, which will take you from London through the 'virtual' English countryside to Hogsmeade Station at The Wizarding World of Harry Potter at Islands of Adventure. (You'll need a two-park ticket to ride the train.)

DINING RESERVATIONS NUMBER

UNIVERSAL THEME PARKS
Tel: 407-224-4012

Revenge of the Mummy: Based on the DreamWorks movie of the same name, this scary rollercoaster ride goes through darkened Egyptian chambers and passageways. For inspiration, Universal developers visited both Egypt and The British Museum in London.

Men in Black: Another ride based on a movie. Shoot the aliens with a laser gun from your vehicle.

Hollywood Rip Ride Rockit: Rollercoaster aimed at the adrenaline junkie – vertical drops, double takes, loops and corkscrews.

The Simpsons Ride (replaces Back to the Future): Go through Krusty Land with Bart, Lisa, Marge and Homer.

Transformers: Prepare for battle alongside the Transformers in this 3-D ride based on the mega movie series, showcasing 15 different Autobots and Decepticons.

UNIVERSAL'S ISLANDS OF ADVENTURE

Parking Garage: 6000 Universal Boulevard, Orlando, 32819
Tel: 407-363-8000. Location: Off the I-4 (after parking your vehicle
at Universal's Parking Garage, walk to the end of CityWalk and it's
on the left) www.UniversalOrlando.com

The other Universal theme park, Islands of Adventure, is filled with vividly painted areas or 'islands,' including...

Seuss Landing: Rides based on Dr Seuss's famous children's books such as The Cat in the Hat.

Jurassic Park: Rides based on the Steven Spielberg classic dinosaur movie of the same name.

Marvel Super Hero Island: With characters such as Captain America, Wolverine, Spider-Man and The Incredible Hulk.

Toon Lagoon: Fun water rides where you can cool down and get splashed.

The Lost Continent: Features shows such as The Eighth Voyage of Sinbad and Poseidon's Fury. Both shows mix live-action with special effects.

Skull Island: Reign of Kong: Board the safari-type vehicle, go through a jungle filled with prehistoric animals, enter the temple gates and fight for your life against the massive King Kong beast. (Opening summer 2016.)

The Wizarding World of HARRY POTTER: Enter the archway of the twenty-acre magical world and discover a Griffindor common room, Hogwarts School, the village of Hogsmeade, and the Hogwart's Express train. (You can board the train at Hogsmeade Station only if you have a park-to-park ticket or Annual Pass.)

TIP The Harry Potter **Escape from Gringots** ride is at the other Universal park: Universal Studios.

Islands of Adventure Highlights

The Wizarding World of Harry Potter: (see above)

Incredible Hulk Coaster: Blasts riders from 0 to 40 mph in two seconds.

Jurassic Park River Adventure: River raft ride with 85-foot plunge.

Dudley Do-Rights Ripsaw Falls: Log flume ride with several watery plunges.

The High in the Sky Seuss Trolley Train Ride!: Nice mild ride great to take young ones on.

The Amazing Adventures of Spider-man: Often voted Orlando's number one ride, the vehicles for the Spiderman ride at Islands of Adventure cost $1 million each to create!

RIDES AT THE WIZARDING WORLD OF HARRY POTTER

Harry Potter and the Forbidden Journey: Fly above Hogwarts in the dark and encounter spiders, scary dementors and a dragon.

Dragon Challenge: An intertwining, twisting rollercoaster.

Flight of the Hippogriff: Family friendly rollercoaster featuring Hagrid's Hut.

SEAWORLD *Sat Nav Address: 7007 SeaWorld Drive, Orlando, 32821. UK Tel: 0800-231-5281. US Tel: 407-351-3600. Location: Central Florida Parkway between International Drive and Sea Harbor Drive. I-Ride Trolley Stop No. 33 South. www.SeaWorldParks.co.uk*
SeaWorld is a marine adventure park packed with numerous species of sea life, including dolphins, whales, stingrays and sharks, all living in multi-thousand gallon viewing tanks.

TIP SeaWorld's dining plan: ALL DAY DINING DEAL. Worth it if your family eats two sit-down meals a day or more and several snacks. Unlimited number of meals. **Note:** Doesn't include the special dining with sharks or any other special event meals.

Bus to Busch Gardens: SeaWorld offers bus transportation to Busch Gardens (BuschGardens.com) theme park, Tampa Bay (free with a purchased Busch Gardens ticket). Call: Shuttle Express Reservations 1-800-221-1339. For a taxi to the shuttle bus, Mears Taxi service, Tel: 407-422-2222. There are a number of bus pickups in Orlando. To find out where they are if you don't want to pay for a taxi, check the website (MearsTransportation.com).

SeaWorld Highlights

Kraken: Named after a mythical sea monster, this tall winding rollercoaster beast reaches speeds of over 65 miles per hour.

Journey to Atlantis: A cross between a rollercoaster and a log flume, this ride ends in a steep drop where the first few seats get soaking wet.

Manta: Facedown ride that glides over sea and sky, then passes through an actual aquarium.

Shamu's Express: Gentle family-friendly ride that drops 800 ft., but at only 28 mph.

DISCOVERY COVE *Sat Nav Address: 6000 Discovery Cove Way, Orlando, 32821. UK Tel: 00800-3344-1818. US Tel: 407-370-1280. Location: Central Florida Parkway between International Drive and Sea Harbor Drive (opposite SeaWorld)*
www.SeaWorldParks.co.uk (click on Discovery Cove) or www.DiscoveryCove.com

Discovery Cove is neither a traditional water park nor a ride-filled theme park, but a tropical oasis where you can interact with dolphins and where, to keep the numbers down, they limit guests to 1000 a day. You can also relax on the man-made beach or explore 'rainforests,' waterfalls, underwater caves, lagoons, artificial reefs teeming with tropical fish, and an aviary with free-flight tropical birds.

Tickets: Are expensive (from roughly $150 to $300 per person, depending on season and package) but considered worth it, particularly for special occasions such as a honeymoons or anniversaries. Included in the price: Parking, all meals and beverages, towels, snorkelling equipment and wet suits/vests, beach umbrellas, lockers and animal-safe sun cream. Just bring your swimming costume [swimsuit] along.

TIP At Discovery Cove, a limited number of special prescription masks are available on a first come, first served basis.

Discovery Cove Bonus: With a Discovery Cove ticket, at time of writing, you'll also receive a 14-day pass to SeaWorld and one for Aquatica Water Park. If you purchase a premium ticket, it also includes Busch Gardens, so that's a nice bonus. However, photographs taken with the dolphins are an extra charge, and so is the experience known as SeaVenture where you walk underwater in a breathable helmet.

Important! To enjoy 'swimming with dolphin' packages at Discovery Cove, you must be at least six years of age. To check in, you'll need a confirmation number and photo I.D. (Telephone first to register or book online.)

LEGOLAND *Sat Nav Address: One LEGOLAND Way, Winter Haven, Polk County, 33884. Tel: US Toll Free: 877-350-LEGO (5346) Location: Roughly an hour's drive southwest of Orlando http://Florida.legoland.com*

Set in 150 acres in Winter Haven, this small park (relative to Disney) is a miniature world of all things Lego, including shows and mild rides. It's geared towards little ones and is absolutely not for thrill seekers, which makes it a nice change if that's what your family are looking for. For an extra charge there's also a water park (check to see if open beforehand) so you may want to pack your children's swim gear. Next door is Cypress Gardens for getting away to the peace and quiet.

Note: Sometimes Legoland closes in the week, so check opening days on website above or call beforehand. Also, all rides stop during a thunderstorm.

Accommodation: Check out Legoland Hotel (http://Florida.legoland.com) if you want to make a day and night of it and arrive early at the park (or Hampton Inn in Winter Haven has a free shuttle service to Legoland, saving you expensive parking fees).

5 WATER PARK TIPS

P opular with families and teens alike, water parks offer a great way to cool-off during Orlando's hot, humid weather. Slides and rides can be extreme and a little scary, others are gently rolling or playful – take your pick.

TIP Disney water parks have free parking, but life vests, inner-tubes, lockers and towels are available to rent.

Note: For details of a luxury tropical beach park, go to: Discovery Cove in the previous THEME PARK TIPS chapter on page 69.

Check First: Go to water-park websites for any height restrictions, opening hours and other current information. Plus, due to capacity constraints or stormy weather or annual renovations, water parks often close for the day. Call ahead to check.

TIP To protect your feet while climbing steps and walking on hot concrete, it's a good idea to wear swim shoes or flip-flops at water parks.

Crowds: In the height of season, water parks are busy and queues for slides can be super long, so arrive early or, if you have a free or discounted ticket, arrive after 3 PM to catch the last few hours. Whatever the time of day or year, water is usually temperature controlled.

Water Park Rules

- No alcohol.

- No glass bottles or containers.

- Proper swimsuits (one-piece swimsuits are recommended for intense slides).

- No metal on swimsuits such as zips or studs.

- Waterproof protectors over nappies [diapers].

DISNEY'S BLIZZARD BEACH *Sat Nav Address: Lake Buena Vista Drive, Lake Buena Vista, 32830. Tel: 407-939-6244. Location: Walt Disney World, off I-4, Exit 65. www.Disneyworld.com*
Disney designed Blizzard Beach to look like a ski-resort with snow-capped, fast plunge slides, as well as kiddie play areas and America's longest raft ride.

Note: To reserve a private patio or lounger with a table, umbrella and towels: Tel: 407-939-7589.

TIP At Blizzard Beach you can pick up a water wallet to protect your money. You'll find them at Snowless Joes, near the entrance.

DISNEY'S TYPHOON LAGOON *Sat Nav Address: 1494*
E. Buena Vista Drive, Lake Buena Vista, 32830. Tel: 407-560-4141. Location: Walt Disney World, off I-4, Exit 67
www.DisneyWorld.com

As the name suggests, Typhoon Lagoon is designed around the effects of a make-believe tropical typhoon. To add atmosphere, there's surfboards dropped in the sand, and a wrecked boat perched on a high rock, as if it's just been tossed from the sea. This water park has a large wave pool, sandy white beach, coral reef, lazy river, nine water slides, and a coaster slide called Crush 'n Gusher that propels riders uphill using water jets.

Note: To reserve a private Beachcomber Shack at Typhoon Lagoon that includes stocked water cooler and towels: Tel: 407-939-7529.

Note: WATER PARK NEWS – UNIVERSAL'S VOLCANO BAY will open 2017. WET 'N WILD will close at end of 2016.

IMPORTANT!

To avoid injuries going down water slides, keep your legs together at all times.

SEAWORLD'S AQUATICA *Sat Nav Address: 5800 Water Play Way, Orlando, 32821. Tel: 407-351-3600. Location: Off Beachline Expressway (528) on International Drive (across from SeaWorld). I-Ride Trolley Stop 34 S. www.SeaWorldParks.co.uk*

Aquatica has a South Seas theme with wave pools, waterfalls and sandy beach. Here you'll find the popular Dolphin Plunge extreme tube slide, where you actually slide past real dolphins (riders must be at least 4-foot high). There's also a fast river ride called Roa's Rapids, as well as Ihu's Breakaway Falls, which is the tallest water ride in the Southern US. For a more leisurely experience, try the raft ride known as Loggerhead Lane. For tiny tots, there's an interactive play fortress called Kata's Kookaburra Cove.

Important! Extra fees for Aquatica's parking, lockers, towels, as well as different luxury levels of private cabanas.

Note: For an indoor surfing pool, go to: Fantasy Surf in OFF THE THEME PARK TRACK chapter on page 139.

6 SHOPPING TIPS

E veryone enjoys a spot of retail therapy, and due to excellent
exchange rates and lower prices, more and more of us
spend at least part of our Orlando trip shopping at the
malls, plazas and discount outlets. With that in mind, this
chapter has bags of shopping tips and advice, a section on size charts,
as well as details on all the popular shopping spots.

Note: For tips on grocery shopping, go to: Shopping for Supplies in
HOLIDAY HOME TIPS chapter on page 34.

Sales Tax: Florida's sales tax rate is only 6 percent. Each retail sale and admission charge is taxable (groceries and medicines are exempt). In addition to the 6 percent state tax, some counties add on a sales surtax. The county tax rate ranges from .5 to 1.5 percent.

Important! Visitors to Florida *cannot* apply for a tax refund on their purchases because the tax charged is not VAT.

CULTURE SHOCK TIP

Question: Why do shoppers pay more at the checkout than the price displayed on the sales tag?

Answer: In America, the price on the shelf does not include sales tax.

Coupons: Enjoy Florida (EnjoyFloridaMagazine.com) is a magazine packed with discount coupons to clothing stores, attractions and restaurants. Look out for other travel-saver magazines available in Orlando that offer savings on hotels and motels. However, remember to read the small print for any extra charges and restrictions.

Excess Baggage: Before you go shopping beware, beware, beware, airport excess baggage charges for additional luggage above your allowance. Extra suitcases cost roughly from £35 to £100 each on long haul flights, depending on the airline. Pack light so you can fill your suitcases for the return flight. Or, as mentioned before, perhaps utilise your children's (not infants) baggage allowance. Don't forget also that any luggage overweight or oversized will also be liable for extra charges. So plan ahead and check with your airline first.

TIP To cut down your stress and guesswork, it's a good idea to invest in a portable luggage-weighing device to weigh your suitcases.

ELECTRONIC ITEMS

American electronic items are 110-120 volt AC. Plugs in hotels and houses are two- and three-pinned, flat pronged, and don't require a fuse. Don't force these plugs into the socket on the wrong side.

IPads, IPods and Laptops: Small items such as IPods and IPads work fine when you take them home (with the right plug adapter). Laptops have variable voltage and work both sides of the pond.

> # WORLDWIDE WARRANTY
>
> Authorized Dealer
> ## For all Apple store products

TIP Supermarkets, electronic stores and airports carry American plug adapters for your British electric shavers, curling irons, hairdryers and other small devices.

Camera and Electronic Stores: There are numerous camera and electronic stores near tourist areas, but beware of the old scam called bait-and-switch. That's where stores entice you in with advertisements offering unbelievably cheap items and then, once you're inside the store, conveniently don't have these items available and try to sell you inflated-priced products instead. These salespeople are experts at the hard-sell, so don't be afraid to walk away and check things out elsewhere.

TIP Best Buy (BestBuy.com) is a large reputable electronic store. There's a branch near Florida Mall *(8001 S. Orange Blossom Trail, 302A, Orlando, 32809. Tel: 407-816-1391)*. Check their website for other store locations.

DVDs: American DVDs are REGION 1. They won't work on British machines, which take REGION 2 (unless you own a two-region player).

CDs: Will work on any players, either side of the pond.

BRITISH NEWSPAPERS

Bookstores such as Barnes and Noble, as well as supermarkets, some hotel receptions [lobbies] and some British-style pubs, often sell British newspapers. The Daily Mail is the only current day paper sold, the rest are one day old. The Union Jack (UJnews.com) local British expat newspaper can be read online or is sold in print form to anyone who signs up and can receive post [mail] to a US address: Sign-up online or Tel: 1-619-466-3129.

SHOPPING MALLS & AREAS

In this section, you'll find details of Orlando's main shopping centres, including the two biggest malls: Florida Mall and the upscale Mall at Millenia. Florida Mall is the most popular. Mall at Millenia is the most stunning but with the most expensive stores. Most popular with Brits are factory outlet shopping malls for discounted clothes, bags, shoes, perfumes, etc., and these are listed later in this chapter.

TIP It's worth heading to customer service desks of shopping malls for store information, currency exchange and coupon books.

Note: Mall stores open around 10 AM. Closing time is roughly 9 PM. On Sundays they open 11 AM and close 6 or 7 PM.

FLORIDA MALL *Sat Nav Address: 8001 S. Orange Blossom Trail, Orlando, 32809. Tel: 407-851-6255*
Location: Corner of Sand Lake Road and S. Orange Blossom Trail
www.Simon.com/mall/the-florida-mall

Most well known in Orlando is Florida Mall, a 2.3 million square foot shopping giant boasting 250 stores, including J.C. Penny department store, Apple, Foot Locker, Gap, and Victoria's Secret. There's free Wi-Fi, plus children's strollers available to rent.

MALL AT MILLENIA *Sat Nav Address: 4200 Conroy Road, Orlando 32839. Tel: 407-363-3555. Location: On Conroy and I-4 www.MallAtMillenia.com*

Mall at Millenia is a shiny, upscale shopping mall, designed with massive video screens and airy, glass-ceiling architecture. There are over 115 luxury stores, including Tiffany's, Bloomingdale's and Gucci.

TIP Mall at Millenia has a full service Post Office, a Mobile Phone [Cell Phone] Charging Station, and is a free Wi-Fi zone.

PARK AVENUE, WINTER PARK *Location: Town of Winter Park, northeast of Orlando; roughly a 40-minute drive from Disney, depending on traffic. www.ExperienceParkAvenue.com*

Park Avenue is a shopping district filled with designer shops, cafes, restaurants, wine bars and chocolatiers, all set in the picturesque tree-lined town of Winter Park. You can take the leisurely boat tour (ScenicBoatTours.com) or if you're in the mood for a film, go to the Regal Cinema or the Enzian Cinema (Note: Cinemas in the US are usually called movie theatres, but in these two cases cinema is their actual name). The Enzian (Enzian.org) is a special place to dine and watch independent art house films in comfort, though you'll probably need to call ahead to book a seat (for more information, go to THE ARTS chapter on page 154).

INTERNATIONAL DRIVE
www.InternationalDriveOrlando.com

International Drive – or I-Drive as it's locally known – is a 12-mile, well-designed winding road that's home to numerous tourist attractions, hotels, restaurants, shopping centres and outlet malls (see Factory Outlets below), and where you'll find **ORLANDO EYE** (OfficialOrlandoEye.com): A new attraction and shopping district anchored by a 400 ft. wheel [Ferris wheel] with capsules to ride in – similar to London Eye – and takes 20 minutes. There's also a Madame Tussauds wax works and a Sea Life aquarium on site.

Trolley Bus: Tel: 407-354-5656, IrideTrolley.com. You can take the I-Ride Trolley, which operates on International Drive, seven days a week from 8 AM to 10.30 PM every 15 minutes. Children under 12 ride free when accompanied by an adult. Pay fare on board with cash or a pass. Passes NOT sold on the trolley but can be purchased on their website or at area hotels. Note: During peak hours, I-Ride Trolleys often fill quickly.

POINTE ORLANDO *Sat Nav Address: 9101 International Drive, Orlando, 32819. Tel: 407-248-2838. Location: Across from Orange County Convention Centre. I-Ride Trolley Stop No. 24 North (and Green No. 12 South) www.PointeOrlando.com*

Pointe Orlando is a pleasant pedestrian centre designed with ponds, landscaping and courtyards. Here you'll find 40 shops, restaurants, nightlife, and a movie multiplex with 3D-IMAX cinema, as well as the dramatic upside-down designed building **WONDERWORKS** (Tel: 407-351-8800, WonderWorksOnline.com) which is an indoor family attraction with interactive games, handy for the family on a rainy afternoon.

WonderWorks

ARTEGON MARKETPLACE *Sat Nav Address: 5250 International Drive, Orlando, 32819. Location: On north end of I-drive. I-Ride Trolley Stop No. 2 North. www.ArtegonOrlando.com*

Located where the old Festival Bay mall stood, Artegon has shops and stalls where artisans display their art and handmade goods. There's also a skate park and a Book Warehouse store. The 20-screen cinema [movie theatre], Ron Jon surfer's store, and Bass Pro Outdoor World sporting goods shop are still in place as before.

FACTORY OUTLETS

Outlet shopping malls are particularly popular with savvy shoppers looking for brand name, upscale items at affordable prices. Some products are seconds, though many are just overstocked or discontinued merchandise from main stores and are good bargains.

ORLANDO PREMIUM OUTLETS on Vineland Ave. *Sat Nav Address: 8200 Vineland Avenue, Orlando, 32821. Tel: 407-238-7787. Location: Off I-4, Exit 68, near SeaWorld. Trolley Stop No. 42 South. www.PremiumOutlets.com*

This Premium Outlet location has over 160 stores, including Tommy Hilfiger, Adidas, Giorgio Armani, Wilson's Leather, and Nike. Convenient free shuttle transportation is offered for guests of Lake Buena Vista area hotels. Reservations: Tel: 407-858-3008.

ORLANDO PREMIUM OUTLETS on International Drive. *Sat Nav Address: 4951 International Drive, Orlando, 32819. Tel: 407-352-9600 Location: North End of International Drive. Trolley Stop 1 North. www.PremiumOutlets.com*

This is the biggest outlet in the area with over 180 brand name stores to shop in, including Reebok, Timberland, Bose, Swarovski, Tommy Hilfiger, and American Eagle Outfitter.

OUTLET MARKETPLACE *Sat Nav Address: 5269 International Drive, Orlando, 32819. Tel: 407-352-9600. Location: Off I-4, Exit 75A. Trolley Stop No. 3 South. www.PremiumOutlets.com*

At this small mall, you'll find 25 outlets, including Calvin Klein, Reebok, Guess, U.S. Polo Assn., and Skechers.

LAKE BUENA VISTA FACTORY STORES *Sat Nav Address: 15657 S. Apopka Vineland Road, Orlando, 32821. Tel: 407-238-9301. Location: Off Highway 192 North. www.LBVFS.com*

Award-winning, Lake Buena Vista Factory Stores have numerous designer and name brands on sale at outlets such as Converse Shoes, Dressbarn, Fossil, Gap, Levi's, Nike, Tommy Hilfiger, Calvin Klein, and Old Navy.

THEME PARK SHOPPING DISTRICTS

 These two free admission theme-park owned districts: **Universal CityWalk** and **Disney Springs** marketplace, are not just for buying theme-park memorabilia but are popular places to hang out, shop, eat and find entertainment (details on their entertainment side can be found in the THEME PARK TIPS chapter on page 55).

UNIVERSAL CITYWALK *Sat Nav Address: 1000 Universal Studios Plaza, Orlando, 32819. Tel: 407-363-8000. Location: I-4 East, Exit 75A; front of Universal Studios www.universalorlando.com/Shopping/CityWalk-Shops.aspx*

CityWalk, known for its varied nightlife and restaurants, has an interesting mix of stores too, including the Quiet Flight surf shop, Hart and Huntington Tattoo Company, and Element for skateboarding apparel and equipment.

DISNEY SPRINGS (formerly Downtown Disney) *Sat Nav Address: Lake Buena Vista, 32830. Tel: 407-824-4321 Location: Off I-4 or off Highway 192 https://disneyworld.disney.go.com/destinations/disney-springs*

Among the many shops here, you'll find the Orlando Harley-Davidson (apparel and accessories) store, Lefty's – The Left Hand Store (tools, gifts and school supplies), a LEGO Imagination Centre with a free kiddie activity playground, World of Disney KIDS for clothes, toys, etc., and a Bibbidi Bobbidi Boutique inside the World of Disney store, Tel: 407-WDW-STYLE (939-7895) – a place where little girls can receive a full princess makeover.

SIZE CHARTS

Below, find comparison charts to UK sizes in clothes and shoes. These are just a rough guide as brands and stores have their own sizes. For instance, Gap have clothes made bigger than average, so you may be an 8 US dress size in Target but only a 6 in the Gap, so it's best to try things on.

TIP Men's suits, trousers [pants], jackets, coats and shirt neck sizes are the same as UK.

WOMEN'S DRESSES AND SUITS										
UK	4	6	8	10	12	14	16	18	20	22
US	2	4	6	8	10	12	14	16	18	20
US LETTER	XS	S	S	M	M	L	L	XL	1X	2X

WOMEN'S JUMPERS [SWEATERS] AND BLOUSES							
UK	34	36	38	40	42	44	46
US	32	34	36	38	40	42	44

WOMEN'S SHOES										
UK	2 ½	3	3 ½	4	4 ½	5	5 ½	6	6 ½	7	7 ½
US	5	5 ½	6	6 ½	7	7 ½	8	8 ½	9	9 ½	10

MEN'S SHOES								
UK	5	6	7	8	9	10	11	12	13
US	6	7	8	9	10	11	12	13	14

CLOTHES SHOPPING TERMS & TRANSLATIONS

BRITISH	AMERICAN
Balaclava	Ski Mask
Braces	Suspenders
Bum Bag	Fanny Pack
Dungarees	Overalls
Handbag	Purse
High-heeled Shoes	Pumps
Jumper	Sweater
Knickers	Panties/Underwear
Lycra	Spandex
Mac or Macintosh	Raincoat
Note (as in money)	Bill (as in dollar bill)
Polo Neck	Turtle Neck
Purse	Wallet (a purse is a handbag)
Queue	Line-up
Shops	Stores/Plazas/Malls/Strip Malls
Suspenders	Garters/Garter Belt
Swimming Costume	Swimsuit
Tights	Pantyhose (tights are wool ones)
Trainers	Sneakers
Trousers	Pants
Trouser Suit	Pant Suit
Turn-ups	Cuffs
Vest	Undershirt
Waistcoat	Vest
Wellington Boots	Rubber Boots

Note: For Grocery Shopping Terms & Translations, go to: HOLIDAY HOME TIPS chapter on page 37.

7 DINING OUT TIPS

Y ou'll find every type of restaurant in Orlando with every type of cuisine, from fine dining to fast food to all-you-can-eat buffets. In this chapter are tips to help you navigate Orlando menus, tips on Disney dining, veggie and health food advice, plus where to find buffets, Indian restaurants, British-style pubs, English breakfasts, and who's serving a spot of luxury afternoon tea.

First, a few tips on how to keep more dollars in your pocket...

Money-Saving Tips

- Orlando restaurants 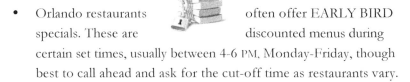 often offer EARLY BIRD specials. These are discounted menus during certain set times, usually between 4-6 PM, Monday-Friday, though best to call ahead and ask for the cut-off time as restaurants vary.

- Some eateries offer KIDS EAT FREE options that can run to a sizeable saving for big families. And due to huge competition, hotels often offer free breakfasts or even senior citizen discounts, so be sure to ask.

- Because portions are so big, except at buffet-style restaurants, it's very acceptable to ask for a take-home container (or doggie bag as it's also called) if you can't finish your meal. In fact, Orlando's serving staff generally encourage this practice, so you can often make two meals out of one (if you have a microwave in your room or villa).

CULTURE SHOCK TIP

Question: Why are restaurant portions so huge in America?

Answer: Food is the cheapest overhead in a restaurant, so over the years, in order to stand out from the competition, plate and portion sizes have grown bigger and bigger. Now Americans expect it.

- Sharing starters [appetizers] and desserts in restaurants is a big money saver. You can replace your main meal [entree] with a couple of appetizers as well. Or, if any young ones don't like the look of the children's menu, they'll often enjoy an appetizer with a dessert to make it a complete meal they can manage.

- If your hotel rate doesn't include breakfast, stock your room with continental breakfast items to save on eating breakfast out. Especially convenient if you have a fridge.

- Drinking free iced water instead of sodas with your meal definitely cuts your restaurant bill down.

- Want to reduce the hotel wine bill? Buy your own wine at an off-licence [liquor store] or supermarket and enjoy it while relaxing on your balcony. To keep wine cool and for mixing other drinks, take advantage of the ice bucket in your room and stock it with ice from the hotel ice machine. In American hotels there's usually an ice machine on every floor. If you're staying at a holiday home, then supermarkets and most petrol [gas] stations sell big bags of ice that you can keep in your freezer.

- At theme parks, instead of dining at expensive restaurants, check your park maps to find sandwich shops, fast food counters and cafes. Sometimes, they're hidden in out-of-the-way corners.

- Also at theme parks, you can bring along your own water bottle and top it up at the free drinking fountains, which are perfectly safe to drink from.

Restaurant Tipping: Portions are huge, service is fast and friendly and prices are usually low; eat well and don't forget to tip. Tipping is in the American culture. Waiters are poorly paid and rely heavily on tips – usual tip is 15% or 20% of the bill [the check]. Remember, you're tipping the service not the food. However, don't double tip – read your bill [your check] first to see if gratuities have already been included before you hand over any more of your hard-earned money.

Note: For other tipping advice: go to Cash For Tipping in KNOW BEFORE YOU GO chapter on page 185.

TIP Automatic gratuities are often added to dining bills [checks] for groups of over six people.

Ordering Food: Americans expect numerous food choices when dining out, and waiters ask lots of questions: 'Do you want it cooked this way or that?' 'Do you want this sauce or that?' 'Do you want this special item or that?' It's all about giving good service and pleasing the customer, so relax and enjoy. It's also okay to modify menu items*. Waiters are used to it. So if you don't want something, say so. For instance, if you don't want cheese on something, ask to 'hold the cheese'. If you want a different vegetable, ask for the options. Occasionally, an exchanged item will cost a little extra, but the waiter will always let you know.

Note: On pages 99 and 105, you'll find a list of menu items explained.

 **BRITISH-STYLE PUBS**

Fancy a taste of England? A British pint? You'll find plenty of Brit-style pubs in the Greater Orlando area if you know where to look, though a few (not mentioned here) are definitely in need of refurbishment. All offer tap beers and have table service; handy if you don't like going to the bar. Most serve British fare, including fish-and-chips, pie-and-chips and Sunday roast dinner. Many televise English league football [soccer] matches and important European ones, but call first to check. On the next page is a list of the more popular pubs.

(By the way, for information on Florida cocktails go to Drinks section on page 109)

Note: The **CRICKETERS ARMS** has now closed.

---

*Exception: Theme park fast-food cafes usually can't change menu items because their food has been pre-prepared at another location.

THE PUB ORLANDO *Sat Nav Address: 9101 International Drive, Suite 1003, Orlando, 32819. Tel: 407-352-2305. Location: Pointe Orlando shopping plaza. I-Ride Trolley Stop No. 24 North (and Green No. 12 South) www.ExperienceThePub.com/Orlando* MODERN, SHINY PUB and 200-guest restaurant with inside and outside dining. You can even sample different types of beer from the 'Pour Your Own Beer Walls'.

HARP AND CELT IRISH PUB & RESTAURANT *Sat Nav Address: 25 S. Magnolia Avenue, Orlando, 32801. Tel: 407-481-2928. Location: Downtown Orlando. www.HarpAndCelt.com* DOWNTOWN PUB lovingly built by Irish owners, with a warm, friendly feel. Visited by President Obama!

GEORGE AND DRAGON *Sat Nav Address: 6314 International Drive, Orlando, 32819. Tel: 407-351-3578. Location: Near the Rosen Inn. Between I-Ride Trolley stops 9 and 10. www.OrlandoGeorgeAndDragon.com* SERVES THE USUAL British food favourites, including best-back bacon for breakfast. Call or check website for times of football matches.

FIDDLER'S GREEN IRISH PUB & EATERY *Sat Nav Address: 544 West Fairbanks Avenue, Winter Park, 32789. Tel: 407-645-2050. Directions to Winter Park: Take I-4 to Fairbanks Avenue Exit in Winter Park. Head East on Fairbanks. At the corner of Fairbanks and Pennsylvania make a right-hand turn (cross over Orange Avenue) and make a left into the car park [parking lot]. www.FiddlersGreenOrlando.com* FORTY-FIVE MINUTE drive from Orlando, this American Automobile Association (AAA) approved pub serves everything from Irish stew to corned beef and cabbage.

RAGLAN ROAD IRISH PUB & RESTAURANT *Sat Nav Address: 1640 East Buena Vista Drive, Lake Buena Vista, 32830 Tel: 407-938-0300. Location: Disney Springs. www.RaglanRoad.com* OFFERS AN inventive menu from the master chef of this authentic Irish-owned pub.

TIP Due to the time difference, don't forget 'live' matches at pubs start five hours after British time.

INDIAN RESTAURANTS

A curry is now a part of our British way of life as much as roast beef and Yorkshire pudding is, so below find a sample of Indian eateries in Orlando to satisfy your weekly fix.

MEMORIES OF INDIA *Sat Nav Address: 7626 Turkey Lake, Orlando, 32819. Tel: 407-370-3277*
www.MemoriesOfIndiaCuisine.com WARM lighting and tasty Indian dishes, this restaurant has a reputation for being one of the best in Orlando.

CULTURE SHOCK TIP
Until chip and pin cards become widespread in America, waiters won't process credit/debit cards at the table. So don't be alarmed when they take your card to the cash register.

WOODLANDS *Sat Nav Address: 6040 S. Orange Blossom Trail, Orlando, 32809. Tel: 407-854-3330 (closed on Mondays)*
www.WoodlandsUSA.com LITTLE-KNOWN GEM, this informal restaurant is great for tasty Southern Indian vegetarian dishes. Note: No alcohol served.

NEW PUNJAB INDIAN RESTAURANT *Sat Nav Address: 7451 International Drive, Orlando, 32819. Tel: 407-352-7887 I-Ride Trolley Stop No. 14 North. www.NewPunjabIndian.com* ESTABLISHED 1981, this restaurant offers a wide variety of Indian food all made fresh daily.

AASHIRWAD *Sat Nav Address: 5748 International Drive, Orlando, 32819. Tel: 407-370-9830. I-Ride Trolley Stop No. 6 N. www.AashirwadRestaurant.com* GOOD PLACE for hot and spicy Tandoori cooking. Open daily (and for lunch buffet).

TABLA BAR AND GRILL *Sat Nav Address: 5827 Caravan Court, Orlando, 32819. Tel: 407-248-9400. www.TablaBar.com* UNUSUAL DISHES offered here, including Indian-Chinese fusion meals.

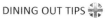

TASTE OF PUNJAB INDIAN RESTAURANT *Sat Nav*
Address: 4980 W. Irlo Bronson Highway, Kissimmee, 34746
Tel: 407-507-3900. www.TasteOfPunjabOrlando.com MID-PRICED
INDIAN RESTAURANT with a wide range of meat and veggie dishes.

CULTURE SHOCK TIP

Servers ask, 'Is it TO GO?' when offering
take-out or take-away services.

VEGGIE OPTIONS

Most restaurants in Orlando offer at least one vegetarian option, and
it's a good idea to ask about these when booking your table.

TIP Indian restaurants have more veggie options than almost any other
type (see Indian Restaurants above).

 DISNEY WORLD VEGGIE OPTIONS

Disney restaurants and cafes have interesting veggie options whatever your
budget. In EPCOT's Morocco pavilion at the **TANGIERINE CAFE** they
serve hummus, lentil salad and falafel. Here's an example from the casual
restaurant, **CAPTAIN'S GRILLE** at Disney's Yacht Club Resort: Sweet
potato tortellini with cranberry relish, spice almonds and brown butter
rosemary beurre blanc. Or Disney will arrange for their chefs to cook a
special meal, if you give them plenty of notice. For example, at time of
writing, the fine dining restaurant **CALIFORNIA GRILL** at Disney's
Contemporary Resort has a popular dish called Vegetarian Unplugged,
comprising of several tasty samples arranged artistically on a big platter. Call
ahead to book and ask if this vegetarian dish is available. If you're lucky and
there's a table for you, you can time your meal to coincide with watching
the nightly Disney fireworks show from the restaurant's panoramic windows.
However, whatever time you dine, you can return to watch the fireworks
from California Grill's lounge or observation deck. Just show your dining
receipt to get back in.

Veggie Eateries

Here's a selection of casual vegetarian places that aren't theme-park owned (some have websites and some don't).

POWER HOUSE CAFE *Sat Nav Address: 111 E. Lyman Avenue, Winter Park, 32789. Tel: 407-645-3616 (closed Sundays) www.PowerHouseCafe.com* POWER HOUSE is good for lunches, sandwiches and wraps.

MELLOW MUSHROOM *Sat Nav Address: 11680 E. Colonial Drive, Orlando, 32817. Tel: 407-384-4455. https://mellowmushroom.com/store/orlando (And in Winter Park: Sat Nav Address: 2015 Alamo Avenue, Winter Park, 32792. Tel: 407-657-7755. https://mellowmushroom.com/store/winter-park)* MELLOW MUSHROOM is famous for its veggie pizzas.

VEGGIE GARDEN *Sat Nav Address: 1216 E. Colonial Drive, Suite 11, Orlando, 32803. Tel: 407-228-1740.* VIETNAMESE VEGAN and veggie cafe that's popular for its big soups.

GARDEN CAFE *Sat Nav Address: 810 W. Colonial Drive, Orlando, 32804. Tel: 407-999-9799.* CHINESE VEGGIE RESTAURANT (even though the menu says meat, they mean fake meat).

ETHOS *Sat Nav Address: 601-B New York Avenue, Winter Park, 32789. Tel: 407-228-3898. www.EthosVeganKitchen.com* AWARD-WINNING, all-vegan restaurant, serving inventive and tasty dishes such as Pecan Encrusted Eggplant, which is a slice of eggplant encrusted with pecans, sautéed and finished with red wine sauce and served with mashed potatoes, gravy and today's veg. Other dishes on the menu include pastas, pizzas, soups and sandwiches. Note: No reservations taken except for parties of over eight people.

TIP For a list of veggie and vegan cafes and restaurants anywhere in America, go to website: HappyCow.net

HEALTH FOODS

CHAMBERLINS MARKET *Town Corral Shopping Center [note American spelling], Sat Nav Address: 1114 N. John Young Parkway, Kissimmee, 34741. Tel: 407-846-7454. www.Chamberlins.com* AS WELL AS the freezer sections of supermarkets, you can shop for veggie and health foods at these small health food stores.

WHOLEFOODS MARKET (see addresses below) sells organic fruits and veggies and healthy food. They also have tasty buffet bars serving both hot and cold veggie (and meat) dishes. There's also a huge selection of wines and cheeses as well as a juice bar for freshly made juices. Wholefoods Markets are so successful they have stores all over America (and a massive one in Kensington, London, UK, if you want to try one out).

WHOLEFOODS LOCATIONS
www.WholeFoods.com
- 8003 Turkey Lake Road, Orlando, 32819. Tel: 407-355-7100
- 1989 Aloma Avenue, Winter Park, 32792. Tel: 407-673-8788

TIP Health stores in America also sell herbal remedies and other holistic products, many at cheaper prices than you'll find in the UK.

 ## ALL-YOU-CAN-EAT BUFFETS

To enjoy a casual eating experience, serve yourself, buffet-style restaurants are popular and good for the whole family (especially for fidgety little ones who can wander around these restaurants, within reason). Orlando has so many buffet restaurants, you'll be spoilt for choice. Be wary though, not all are created equal. A packed car park [parking lot] is usually an indication of a good reputation. If you're still not sure, ask to have a look at the buffet before committing to a reservation. Take a quick peek to see if your group will like the dishes on offer and that the water under the food terrines is steaming; a sign the food is kept hot enough for food safety reasons.

Types of Buffet: Many of the Indian restaurants listed above also offer a buffet (usually at lunchtime), so be sure to ask if that's what you're looking for. Below is a sample of other types. There's Chinese for the budget conscious, steak buffets for meat lovers, and hotel buffets for excellent quality but at higher prices. Also mentioned is Sweet Tomatoes, who have so many interesting dishes they will change your mind about salads not being filling or interesting enough.

Note: For buffets that include a show, go to: Dinner Shows in OFF THE THEME PARK TRACK chapter on page 144.

TIP Lunch buffet menus are cheaper than dinner ones. Some restaurants change prices late afternoon, so be sure to check first.

Chinese Buffets

WILD RICE BUFFET *Sat Nav Address: 843 Lee Road, Orlando, 32810. Tel: 407-628-0088 www.Wildricebuffet.com*

NEW YORK CHINA BUFFET *Sat Nav Address: 12173 S. Apopka Vineland Road, Orlando, 32836. Tel: 407-238-9198.*

KIM WU CHINESE RESTAURANT *(small lunchtime only buffet, 10 AM to 3:30 PM) Sat Nav Address: 4904 S. Kirkman Road, Orlando, 32811. Tel: 407-293-0752.*

TIP Two Chinese restaurants with good reputations that are NOT buffet: P. F. Chang's (PFChangs.com) and Ming Court (Ming-Court.com).

Steak Buffets

PONDEROSA (see addresses below). Ponderosa's steak main course [entrée] comes with an all-you-can-eat cheap and cheerful buffet. They also have a very reasonably priced breakfast buffet.

PONDEROSA LOCATIONS
http://PonderosaSteakHouses.com

- 6362 International Drive, Orlando, 32819 (I-Ride Trolley Stop No. 10 North) Tel: 407-352-9343
- 8510 International Drive, Orlando, 32819 (I-Ride Trolley Stop No. 20 South) Tel: 407-354-1477
- 7598 W. Irlo Bronson Highway, Kissimmee, 34747. Tel: 407-396-7721
- 5771 W. Irlo Bronson Highway, Kissimmee, 34746 (across from Old Town) Tel: 407-397-2100

TIP For a medium-priced steak restaurant chain that is NOT buffet, you might like to try a **Longhorn Steakhouse** (LongHornSteakhouse.com).

Salad Buffets

SWEET TOMATOES For a healthy and tasty mid-priced alternative, you can't go far wrong at Sweet Tomatoes (called Soup Plantation in some US states, hence their website name below). This is salad like you've never seen, with dozens of delicious options.* They also serve all-you-can-eat pastas, soups and desserts.

SWEET TOMATOES LOCATIONS
www.Souplantation.com

- Colonial Promenade, 4678 East Colonial Drive, Orlando, 32803. Tel: 407-896-8770
- 3236 Rolling Oaks Blvd., Kissimmee, 34747. Tel: 407-465-0023
- 12561 S. Apopka-Vineland Road, Orlando, 32836. Tel: 407-938-9461
- International Festival, 6877 South Kirkman Road, Orlando, 32819. Tel: 407-363-3636

*The salad bar price at Sweet Tomatoes is for one-time serve only, but you can have as much as you like of everything else.

Upscale Hotel Buffets

It's great to splurge on dining at hotels, especially for meals such as breakfast or buffets or Sunday brunch, and the nice thing about Florida is you're always welcome to dine, even if you're not a guest of a hotel. The resorts listed below are fun and interesting to explore, too.

Important! Make sure you book a hotel restaurant reservation first.

Note: The famous Sunday Brunch at **LA COQUINA RESTAURANT** at the Hyatt Regency Grand Cypress Resort is not available anymore.

BOMA – FLAVORS OF AFRICA at **Disney's Animal Kingdom Lodge.** *Sat Nav Address: 2901 Osceola Parkway, Lake Buena Vista, 32830. Tel: 407-938-3000.*
https://disneyworld.disney.go.com/resorts/animal-kingdom-lodge
THE EXCELLENT AFRICAN themed Boma buffet is offered every evening at Disney's Animal Kingdom Lodge hotel. Be adventurous here, as each dish is a feast for the senses. And be sure to explore this impressive hotel both inside and out. You'll find African animals in the grounds, which is a great way to round off your evening.

VILLA DE FLORA at **Gaylord Palms Hotel.** *Sat Nav Address: 600 West Osceola Parkway, Kissimmee, 34746. Tel: 407-586-2000 Sunday Brunch 12-3 PM. www.GaylordHotels.com* ANOTHER FINE-DINING restaurant, though Villa de Flora's Sunday Brunch has a Mediterranean-themed menu and is set in a luscious tropical setting at the Gaylord Palms Hotel. After, you can stroll around the immense 4.5-acre glass-enclosed atrium, depicting Floridian regions such as Key West, St. Augustine, and the gator-infested Everglades.

THE BOHEME RESTAURANT at **Grand Bohemian Hotel.** *Sat Nav Address: 325 S. Orange Avenue, Orlando, 32801. Tel: 407-313-9000. Sunday Brunch 10 AM-2 PM (except holidays). www.GrandBohemianHotel.com* IF YOU enjoy the finer things in life, then treat yourself to the Sunday Jazz Brunch in this artsy downtown Orlando hotel.

Buffet Etiquette

When dining at an American buffet restaurant, pick up a clean plate for each trip to the food counters. Leave your cutlery [silverware] and used plate on the table. Your server will clear away your plate but will leave your cutlery [silverware] for your return if they are left on the table and not on your plate.

 BREAKFASTS

If you enjoy a traditional breakfast and you're not staying at a hotel serving affordable or inclusive full breakfasts, then you may like to try dining at one of these cheap and cheerful American budget diner franchises: IHOP (International House of Pancakes), Golden Corral, Denny's, Cracker Barrel, Sizzler or Ponderosa. (See Steak Buffets on page 95 for locations of Ponderosa)

DENNY'S (Dennys.com)

440 S. Semoran Blvd., Orlando, 32807
5825 International Drive, Orlando, 32819
7660 International Drive, Orlando, 32819
8747 International Drive, Orlando, 32819
11037 International Drive, Orlando, 32821
8076 S. Orange Ave., Orlando, 32809
8243 S. John Young Parkway, Orlando, 32819
3957 S. Kirkman Rd., Orlando, 32811
2509 W. Vine St., Kissimmee, 34741
2051 E. Irlo Bronson Hwy., Kissimmee, 34744
1515 E. Osceola Parkway, Kissimmee, 34744
5855 W. Irlo Bronson Hwy., Kissimmee, 34746
4783 W. Irlo Bronson Hwy., Kissimmee, 34746

More diners on next page . . .

IHOP (IHOP.com)

647 East Colonial Drive, Orlando, 32803

7661 International Drive, Orlando, 32819

9990 International Drive, Orlando, 32819

6005 International Drive, Orlando, 32819

7693 S. Orange Blossom Trail, Orlando, 32809

5203 Kirkman Rd., Orlando, 32819

5184 W. Spacecoast Parkway, Kissimmee, 34746

6065 W. Irlo Bronson Hwy., Kissimmee, 34747

7529 W. Irlo Bronson Hwy., Kissimmee, 34746

1715 West Vine St., Kissimmee, 34741

GOLDEN CORRAL (GoldenCorral.com)

5535 S. Kirkman Rd., Orlando, 32819

8032 International Drive, Orlando, 32819

8707 Vineland Ave, Orlando, 32821

6077 W. Irlo Bronson Hwy., Celebration, 34747

7702 W. Irlo Bronson Hwy., Kissimmee, 34747

2701 W. Vine St, Kissimmee, 34741

11731 E. Colonial Drive, Orlando, 32817

7251 West Colonial Drive, Orlando, 32818

2328 S. Semoran Blvd., Orlando, 32822

SIZZLER (Sizzler.com)

9142 South International Drive, Orlando, 32819

12195 S. Apopka Vineland, Orlando, 32819

7602 Irlo Bronson Hwy., Kissimmee, 34741

CRACKER BARREL (CrackerBarrel.com)

5400 W. Irlo Bronson Hwy., Kissimmee, 34746

7878 W. Irlo Bronson Hwy., Kissimmee, 34747

6699 South Semoran Blvd., Orlando, 32822

13300 S. Orange Blossom Trail, Orlando, 32837

Breakfast Menu Items

American Bacon: American bacon consists of crispy strips of the streaky variety. Best-back bacon is rarely available in Orlando's restaurants. (Canadian bacon is the closest to best-back in North America).

Sausages: Breakfast sausages are sometimes called links. You may also be served a round sausage, known as a sausage patty.

Ordering Eggs: Eggs come fried in a variety of ways, and you'll be asked how you'd like them cooked. Here are the options:

SUNNY-SIDE UP (fried on one side)

OVER-EASY (fried lightly on both sides)

OVER-MEDIUM (fried on both sides a bit longer than over-easy)

Omelettes: Some hotels have omelette stations serviced by a chef. The chef will ask you to choose your omelette's ingredients from the selection displayed.

Pancakes: American pancakes are thick (unlike crepes) and are popular served with maple syrup. They can be made with blueberries or topped with cream and fruit such as strawberries. Pancakes with maple syrup usually come with a dollop of butter on top. Tell the waiter if you don't want the butter.

'WOULD YOU LIKE HALF-AND-HALF?'

Half-and-half means cream for your coffee, which is half milk, half cream.

Hash Browns: Finely cut fried potatoes, especially delicious at Cracker Barrel restaurants where they come cooked in cheese (see above).

Toast: In many restaurants toast comes already buttered. If you don't like it this way, order the butter on the side.

Note: For other menu items explained, go to page 105.

TEA/AFTERNOON TEA

America is a nation of coffee drinkers. Finding a good cup of tea is practically impossible. That's why tea bags are the number one item we Brits like to tuck inside our suitcase.

Ordering Tea: When you ask for a tea in an American eatery or cafe, you'll probably be given a cup of hot water and a tea bag for dipping. Sometimes tea comes with lemon only, so ask for milk if preferred (often you're given a coffee creamer by mistake). The server will ask you what type of tea you'd like, as restaurants and cafes offer many varieties including herbal and other speciality teas. If in doubt, ask for English or English Breakfast.

TIP Iced tea is popular, especially in the heat of the summer, so remember to ask for hot tea if that's what you want.

DID YOU KNOW?

Americans invented the Tea Bag.

Where to Buy Black Tea: Tea varieties available in the US tend to be weaker in flavour. British tea bags can be purchased in the English section at many Publix supermarkets, and at these two stores:

BRITISH SUPERMARKET, *5695 Vineland Road, Orlando (close to Universal Studios) Tel: 407-370-2023*

THE BRITISH SHOPPE, *809 N. Mills Avenue, Orlando, 32803 Tel: 407-898-1634. www.TheBritishShoppe.com*

100

Luxury Afternoon Tea Spots

Fancy a spot of afternoon tea the old-fashioned way, with all the trimmings: cakes, sandwiches, and even Champagne? Check out the following (prices are from $15-$50 per person, depending on venue).

TIP Suggested dress code for luxury afternoon tea: casually elegant.

GARDEN VIEW TEA ROOM at **Disney's Grand Floridian Resort**
Sat Nav Address: 4401 Floridian Way, Lake Buena Vista, 32830
Tel: 407-WDW-DINE (939-3463). Afternoon Tea: Between 2 PM to 4.30 PM daily. www.DisneyWorld.com HERE YOU'LL DISCOVER a sunny tea room decorated in cool whites, where speciality teas in fine china are served with sandwiches, cakes and strawberries and cream. Extremely busy on Mother's Day (the American one is celebrated on the second Sunday in May) and Christmas, and other holidays, so book well in advance.

THE LOBBY LOUNGE at **Ritz-Carlton Orlando at Grande Lakes**
Sat Nav Address: 4012 Central Florida Parkway, Orlando, 32837
Tel: 407-393-4034. Afternoon Tea: Saturday and Sunday between 2-4 PM. www.GrandeLakes.com CHOOSE FROM the standard afternoon tea, Royal Tea or a Peter Rabbit Tea for children. The Royal Tea includes a glass of Champagne, and the cream with the strawberries is whipped with a hint of Grand Marnier. Reservations are required at least 24-hours in advance.

MAGNOLIA TERRACE TEA ROOM & RESTAURANT
Sat Nav Address: 6282 Commercial Way, Weeki Wachee, 34613
Tel: 1-352-556-4819. Afternoon Tea: Monday to Saturday
www.MagnoliaTerraceTearoom.com THIS ELEGANT TEA ROOM is especially useful if you're in the area to see the Weeki Wachee Spring mermaid show (page 135 for details).

PARK PLAZA GARDENS RESTAURANT *Sat Nav Address: 319 Park Avenue South, Winter Park, 32789. Tel: 407-645-2475 Royal Tea: Fridays. http://parkplazagardens.com/high-tea-champagne-on-the-avenue* IF YOU'RE IN the Winter Park area on a Friday, why not go for a Royal Tea with Champagne at this lovely upscale restaurant.

DISNEY DINING

Note: See also Disney Dining Plans later in this chapter.

Booking a Table: You can book up to 180 days before your trip (if you're a Disney hotel guest) or 180 days before your dining reservation, if not.

- Tel: 407-WDW-DINE (939-3463).

- Or dial the special UK Disney number: Tel: 0870-242-4900.

- Or book online at:
  https://disneyworld.disney.go.com/dining/#/reservations-accepted

- Or if you're already at a Disney theme park, you can book a table from any of the Guest Relations' desks or at the individual restaurants.

Disney's reservation system is called **Advanced Dining Reservations** (previously called Priority Seating). Here's the lowdown...

- Disney restaurants won't keep a table empty for you, but you'll get the next available table at the time of your reservation. You may still have to wait awhile, though it's usually a lot quicker than just turning up and risk being turned away.

- It is highly recommended that you use this system, especially during school holidays and peak times, such as Christmas, Easter, Forth of July, Valentine's Day, Mother's Day (American Mother's Day is the second Sunday in May), and Thanksgiving (fourth Thursday in November). Many restaurants are booked months in advance.

- If, however, you suddenly decide you want to dine at a popular restaurant, it's actually better to call ahead (Tel: 407-939-3463) rather than just turn up at the door – even if it's only 10 minutes ahead of time.

- It's really important to book ahead if you want you and your children to dine with Disney characters.

TIP A $10 cancellation fee for some Disney table service restaurants will be charged if you leave it too late or are a no show. You can cancel your dining reservation online or by calling 407-WDW-DINE (939-3463) up to 11:59 PM Eastern Time on the day before your arrival at the restaurant.

Important! Children under 10 are not allowed at Victoria and Albert's in the Grand Floridian Resort and Spa. Plus, this is the only Disney restaurant with a dress code: Men: jackets. Women: dresses or trouser suits [pant suits].

Disney Princess Dining

Dining with Cinderella and the other Disney princesses at the Royal Table at Magic Kingdom is another story and practically impossible to book for. Here are the steps at time of writing...

1. You can book in advance on the first day you're permitted to call (up to 180 days before your reservation*). All 150 tables are usually booked in the first few minutes of availability, so this is important.

2. Have your credit card ready as, unlike most Disney dining reservations, you'll need to pay in full for dining at the Royal Table beforehand. Be flexible on times and dates.

3. If you don't get booked, try again in the hope there's been a cancellation. If not, ask if there are other options to dine or see princess characters.

4. You'll be given a confirmation number. Bring this with you. After all the trouble of booking, you don't want to discover there's a problem with your reservation.

*Disney hotel guests can calculate day of booking restaurant from first day of hotel stay (not the day of the reservation). This gives hotel guests a few days advantage over other bookers.

Disney Dining Plans
www.DisneyWorld.com

If you're booking a Disney Vacation Package (or Magic Your Way Vacation Package) then you may be lucky enough to be offered a free dining plan as part of a promotion. If not, then you can pay for a dining plan to be added to your package. There are different levels of Disney Dining Plans and none of them are inexpensive, even the Quick Service Dining option, which at time of writing is over $40 per person per day. However, you may find them convenient to use and they may even help you budget your holiday.

How Disney Dining Plans Work: Each day you are given credits to use at the restaurants or cafes in your plan. When you receive your meal receipt, it will tell you how many credits you have left for the day. The amount of money you save depends on the cost of meal you order. In other words, you may purchase a meal from, say, the Deluxe Plan for $20, or one at $50 for the same credit.

TIP For sing-a-long breakfasts with Disney characters, dine at Chef Mickey's Fun Time Buffet, 4th floor of Disney's Contemporary Resort.

Are Dining Plans Worth It?: Some people love these plans and some people don't. The people who do, have families who like to spend time at sit-down, table service restaurants eating big meals. The people who don't are those with families who don't want to be tied down to restaurant reservations or who eat small meals. Also, using a dining plan takes quite a bit of pre-planning and booking and if you don't want the bother, then it's not for you. But then again, that's what cold winter evenings are for – planning your hols in the sun.

TIP Universal (UniversalOrlando.com) also has a (straight forward) holiday [vacation] dining plan to use at over 100 theme park and CityWalk eateries.

MENU ITEMS

Note: For American breakfast foods explained, go to Breakfast Menu Items on page 99.

Starters: Starters are called **appetizers.** Many people like appetizers so much they order two or three for their main meal [entrée]. As mentioned before, this is also a good idea if children can't find anything else they like on the menu.

Salads: Orlando restaurants often have great salad bars – some are even all-you-can-eat. When ordering a salad off a regular menu, you'll be asked what dressing you'd prefer. Restaurants have several types, including French, Ranch, Thousand Island, Balsamic, Blue Cheese and Italian. Note: Salad Cream is unavailable at restaurants but can be bought at some supermarkets in the 'Ethnic Aisle'.

Potatoes: A jacket potato is called a **baked potato** and comes with choice of toppings: sour cream, chives, bacon bits, butter and/or cheese. Smashed potato is mashed potato roughly done, usually with the skin left on.

CULTURE SHOCK TIP

Crisps are called Chips
Chips are called Fries

TIP Except for fish 'n chips, if you see a menu item that say it comes with chips, it usually means crisps. Ask for fries if that's what you want.

Prawns: Are called **shrimps** and are usually king size. Small ones are called baby shrimp.

Conch: (pronounced Conk). Comes from seashells. You'll often see conch fritters on the menu at seafood restaurants, usually served with seafood dipping sauce.

TIP Bahama Breeze is a seafood restaurant chain with a consistently good reputation. They have five locations in the Greater Orlando area. Go to: BahamaBreeze.com for further details.

Popcorn: Popcorn is the salted/buttered variety; there's no sweet popcorn, but you can buy caramel popcorn at the supermarkets and petrol stations [gas stations].

Buffalo Wings: Are chicken wings smothered in barbeque sauce.

Grits: An acquired taste, grits are mushy breakfast food made of corn meal.

Biscuits and Gravy: Biscuits, slightly salty in flavour, are similar to savoury scones. Popular either buttered or served on the side with gravy. (If you want the type of biscuit you eat with your cuppa, ask for a cookie.)

Corn Bread: Made of cornmeal, and with a cake-like texture, corn bread is usually served with soups or deep-fried chicken.

Corn Dogs: These are hot dogs made of corn instead of meat products.

Chilli Dogs: Hot dogs smothered in chilli con carne.

English Muffins: Similar to crumpets but more doughy. Usually toasted and spread with butter and/or jam.

(Soft) Pretzels: Found in various sizes and twisted into a looped knot, a soft pretzel is made of dough and sprinkled with coarse salt.

Sandwiches: Ordering quickly at a delicatessen (or deli) counter or cafe can be a bit daunting until you know what your preferences are. Of course, Americans are a dab hand at this: 'I'll have a BLT toasted on whole-wheat with mustard and hold the mayo'.

- Or in a submarine shop: 'I'll have a six inch meatball sub, Italian bread, spicy mustard, American cheese, everything on'.

- Often in cafes, you can have your filling on a croissant, a bagel or a roll. The term 'roll' is used instead of 'bun' (except at McDonalds and other burger joints).

- Maybe you'd like that toasted or plain, with or without mayo or honey-mustard sauce? Pickle? Oil and vinegar?

Well you get the idea, the list is endless. We still sometimes have trouble being understood just ordering a tuna sandwich if we pronounce it the British way 'choona' instead of the American way 'toona'.

TIP The pickle in a sandwich is a slice of big gherkin.

Bread: Whole-wheat (brown) bread is popular, but you can also choose from white, honey-wheat, sourdough, and rye, to name a few. By the way, Americans never butter sandwich bread unless you ask them to.

Melt: A sandwich smothered in hot melted cheese is called a melt.

Club: A club sandwich is a double or triple-decker layered sandwich.

Corned Beef: Is not the tinned [canned] style eaten in the UK, but a kind of cured, salted beef that tastes completely different.

TIP For road trips and picnics in the summer sun, it's a good idea to pick up an inexpensive Styrofoam cooler box and fill it with ice to keep your food fresh. Both the cooler and large bags of ice can be bought from supermarkets or petrol [gas] station.

DESSERTS & CAKES

Warning! Reading this section will make you go put the kettle on and eat something delicious.

Desserts such as chocolate brownies and carrot cake have made their way to Britain. Here are some others you may come across in Florida:

Coffee Cake: You may be forgiven for thinking a coffee cake is a cake flavoured with coffee. It isn't, it's just plain old cake to drink with your cup of coffee.

Pound Cake: Also popular with a cup of coffee is a slice of pound cake, which is like a Madeira cake.

Upside-down Cake: Usually pineapple. Made in a pan with the fruit on the bottom and then, once baked, turned upside down.

TIP Disney special occasion cakes are available for an additional charge, and are ordered 72 hours in advance by calling Tel: 407-827-2253. For more celebration extras: https://disneyworld.disney.go.com/celebrations/customizations

Key Lime Pie (also available in the UK): A popular southern dessert. This pie is made of limes, tastes tart, has a graham cracker crust (similar to digestive biscuits) and is sometimes topped with whipped cream.

Cobbler: You won't find any fruit crumble desserts in America, but you will find this similar baked type. Delicious served with ice cream.

Jelly Roll: Is a Swiss roll with jam [jelly] in the middle.

Apple Brown Betty: Dessert made with baked apples, brown sugar and breadcrumbs.

Boston Cream Pie: Not a pie at all, but a cake with yellow custard filling and chocolate icing. You can buy Boston cream doughnuts too.

Ice Cream: You'll discover dozens of varieties of ice cream in America, such as Rocky Road (chocolate ice cream mixed with nuts and marshmallow), Butter Pecan (a pecan is a type of nut), Peanut Butter, Chocolate Fudge, and many others. Often, frozen yogurt and sorbets are on sale as well as ice cream. People who are lactose intolerant sometimes find these easier to digest.

CULTURE SHOCK TIP

Pie à la mode means pie with ice cream
e.g. apple pie à la mode

Ice Cream Chains: Orlando has excellent ice-cream stores, such as Häagen-Dazs, Ben and Jerry's, and Cold Stone Creamery. It's okay to ask for a small sample if you want to taste a flavour. Check the counters for examples of cone (type and size) available. Or, you can have ice cream in a paper cup.

TIP Hundred and Thousands are called Sprinkles in America.

 DRINKS

Water: In most restaurants iced-water is served first and comes free with the meal, unless you request bottled. The term mineral water is not often used – just request bottled. And don't say still water, it's called non-carbonated.

TIP In full service restaurants, sodas, tea and coffee are sometimes free to top-up. Check the menu first.

Pop: Is called soda, and you won't easily find orange squash (except in the British section of some Florida supermarkets). Although there is concentrated juice in the frozen section of supermarkets.

Alcohol: You must be twenty-one or older to purchase alcoholic drinks in Florida: Carry photo identification [ID] with you for proof of age (even if you look over twenty-one), or you may be denied.

CULTURE SHOCK TIP

Off Licences are called Liquor Stores

Can I take your order, please?: In restaurants, there's no need to order your drinks at the bar unless you want to. A waitress will take your drinks order at the table. (This is why Americans, when new to visiting Britain, sit and wait and wait to be served in a pub.)

"Beer is proof God loves us and wants us to be happy."
Benjamin Franklin
(A Founding Father of America)

Beer: A common complaint from some British drinkers is the type of draft beer available in the US, which to a Brit tastes like lager. (Go to: British-Style Pubs on page 88 to find places that serve British ale.)

Talking of beer, here are some of the popular alcoholic brands offered...

- **US Domestic:** Budweiser (or Bud), Miller, Coors, Shocktop and Amstell. Beers come either light or regular.

- **Imported:** Heineken, Becks, Corona, Woodpecker, Strongbow, Fosters, Boddingtons and Guinness.

Mixed drinks: Drinks such as whiskey and dry ginger are called Highballs. If you ask for a mixed drink like vodka and orange, the orange will be real orange juice not orange squash.

Cocktails:

- A common summer cocktail is a **DAIQUIRI,** which is made with rum and fruit such as strawberries or raspberries, then mixed together in a blender with crushed ice. You can also have an alcohol-free Daiquiri, known as a Virgin Daiquiri.

- A Bucks Fizz (champagne and orange juice) is called a **MIMOSA.**

- For a non-alcoholic cocktail that children love, ask for a **SHIRLEY TEMPLE,** which is a tall glass filled with ice, topped with Sprite or 7-UP, ginger ale, a dash of grenadine and a cherry for garnish.

- Martinis are the James Bond style drink made with gin. Ask for a **VERMOUTH** (pronounced Vermooth) if you want the fortified wine type.

TIP Drinks usually come filled with lots of ice. Ask for a drink 'straight up' or 'no ice' if you don't want ice.

DINING OUT TERMS & TRANSLATIONS

BRITISH	AMERICAN
Aubergine	Eggplant
Beetroot	Beets
Bill (The)	Check (The)
Biscuits	Cookies
Bucks Fizz	Mimosa
Hot Dog (in chilli con carne)	Chilli Dog
Chips	French Fries (or just Fries)
Courgettes	Zucchini
Crisps	Chips
Cutlery	Silverware

111

BRITISH	AMERICAN
Double Cream	Heavy or Whipping Cream
Fish Fingers	Fish Sticks
Gammon	Cured Ham
Grilled	Broiled (or Grilled)
Head Waiter	Maître d'
Hundreds and Thousands	Sprinkles
Identification	ID
Jacket Potato	Baked Potato
Jelly	Jell-O
Joint (of meat)	Roast (or Pot Roast)
Lemonade Pop	Sprite/7-Up/Lemon-Lime Soda
Madeira Cake	Pound Cake (similar to)
Mineral Water	Bottled Water (or Non-Carbonated Water)
Gherkin	Pickle
Pop	Soda
Porridge	Oatmeal
Prawns	Shrimp (small prawns are called Baby Shrimp)
Runner Beans	Green Beans (or String Beans)
Salad Cream	Mayonnaise or Mayo
Salt Cellar	Salt Shaker
Serviette	Napkin
Side Dishes	Sides
Skimmed Milk	1% or 2% Milk (or less)
Spring Onion	Green Onion
Squash	Concentrated Juice
Starters	Appetizers
Still Drink	Non-carbonated
Sweets	Candy
Takeaway	Take Out (or To Go)
With ice cream	À la mode

8 DRIVING TIPS

T he folks at the US Department of Highway Safety and Motor Vehicles will tell you we British are first-class drivers with a reputation for being courteous. Generally speaking, we're considerate of others and we know the rules of the road. These driving skillsets are instilled in us, not to mention our high standard of driving instruction. But it always amazes us that car hire [rental] companies just hand the keys over to visitors without letting drivers know what to expect on the road. So to cut down on stress levels, this chapter deals with car hire, navigation, safety tips, motorways, traffic signs, school buses, tollbooths, police procedures, as well as how to drive an automatic.

TO HIRE [rent] A CAR OR NOT?

If you're staying at a theme park resort or hotel along International Drive, then you can perhaps get by without hiring a car. However, it is virtually impossible to navigate Greater Orlando without a car. Remember, you are coming from a culture that encourages walking, to a culture that (unintentionally) discourages it. And, due to the design and mega size of America, the distances between places are vast.

If you decide *not* to hire [rent] a car, then to get around you must use hotel shuttle buses, theme-park transport, taxies, car services, or catch the Lynx public bus (see below).

After weighing up all the alternative transport options, if you decide to hire a car, the good news is petrol [gas] is at least half the British price.

TIP Here's a website for Brits thinking of renting a car: USrentacar.co.uk

Note: For a list of taxi telephone numbers, go to HANDY PHONE NUMBERS & WEBSITES at the end of this book.

Public Buses: Lynx Buses (Tel: 407-841-5969, GoLynx.com). Public buses are clean, air-conditioned and comfortable, but you sometimes have to wait a long time for one (unpleasant in the heat) and they can take a while to reach your destination, especially if you have to transfer buses.

Theme Park Transport: For park hopping, Disney has free buses, boats and monorails to and within their parks. However, Universal Studios is next door to Islands of Adventure and within walking distance of each other, and the Hogwarts Express train links the two if you have a two-park ticket or are staying at a Universal resort.

Trolley Bus: If your hotel is on International Drive, then you can take advantage of the I-Ride Trolley (Tel: 407-248-9590, IrideTrolley.com). However, when busy, the I-Ride Trolley is often full by the time it gets to your stop.

CAR HIRE [rental] COMPANIES

Hire [Rental] Company	UK Web & Phone	US Web & Phone
Alamo	www.alamo.co.uk Tel: 0870-400-4562	www.alamo.com Tel: 1-800-462-5266
Avis	www.avis.co.uk Tel: 0844-581-0147	www.avis.com 1-800-331-1212
Budget	www.budget.co.uk Tel: 0844-544-3439	www.budget.com Tel: 1-800-527-0700
Dollar	www.dollar.co.uk Tel: 0203-468-7685	www.dollar.com 1-800-800-4000
Enterprise	www.enterprise.co.uk Tel: 0800-800-227	www.enterprise.com Tel: 1-800-261-7331
Hertz	www.hertz.co.uk Tel: 0843-309-3099	www.hertz.com Tel: 1-800-654-3131
Thrifty	www.thrifty.co.uk Tel: 0203 468 7686	www.thrifty.com 1-800-847-4389

TIP You can often hire [rent] a car through your holiday company, sometimes at very favourable rates.

Age Restrictions: You must be twenty-one or over to hire [rent] a car in Florida (many require you to be twenty-five). However, if you are 25 and under, the price of insurance is usually higher, so check first if they have special offers for young drivers.

Types of Vehicle: There are many types of vehicle, such as economy, compact, full size and luxury. If you wish to hire a people carrier or MPV (Multi-Purpose Vehicle) this is called a **MINIVAN** in the US.

Booking: Most people reserve a car before their trip, but if you wait until you're in Orlando it is essential to shop around as prices vary. See handy table above for rental companies. You can sometimes save money by including a car when booking your flight online or as part of a package deal.

Here are some other booking tips ...

- Booking a car online prior to your trip is a good idea and saves waiting in long queues. And don't worry if you change your mind or find another, cheaper agency. You can usually cancel at no charge. This means you can cancel and re-book at the same place if they suddenly have a special sale. Don't forget to print out your agreement and take it with you.

- When signing your contract, watch what you agree to. When they offer you certain packages, ask for an exact breakdown on what you are getting. Car hire [rental] companies make their money by the extra charges they try to load on. For instance, you may already be covered for third-party insurance on your credit card, so check before paying twice. Or maybe your own car insurance covers hire cars [rental cars].

- You can book in advance child safety seats, which are mandatory for children three and under or who weigh 40 lbs. or less. Be sure to check what these seats cost as different companies have variable rates.

- Credit cards are the preferred mode of payment but most rental companies will now accept debit cards with certain terms and conditions, and a cash hold equal to the cost of the rental, plus an extra discretionary amount to cover such eventualities as unpaid tolls, parking fees or damage not covered by insurance, etc. When paying with a debit card you may also need proof of your round-trip ticket.

Pick Up: When picking up your vehicle, sometimes companies try to upgrade you by scaring you into thinking that your car isn't big enough for your family and all your luggage, etc. This sometimes means that they haven't got your size car available and are trying to save themselves upgrading you for free. However, don't expect a seven-seater vehicle to accommodate seven people with seven pieces of luggage, pushchair [stroller], kiddie seat, etc. Pay the extra and hire the vehicle size you need, or be prepared to squeeze in suitcases on or beside seats.

TIP When you pick up your vehicle, if it has any noticeable damage, take a photograph. It may come in handy as evidence if you have to dispute any charges later.

Arrival Time: If you arrive at the airport after dark, then it's a good idea to stay overnight at an airport hotel so you can start the next day fresh in daylight, when it's easier to navigate the roads. Also if you arrive at dusk, by the time you have gone through Immigration, collected your suitcases and picked up your car, it may now be dark. Driving in the dark the moment you arrive in a strange place is not advisable. There are deep ditches at the side of the roads in Florida to avoid. You may find yourself taking the wrong road and getting lost. Being lost, tired and frightened, unable to find your hotel or villa is not a good start to your holiday [vacation]. Another option is to catch an airport shuttle (if your hotel provides one) or take a taxi and have your hire car delivered to your hotel or villa.

TIP CAR ON THE DRIVE (Tel: 407-504-1243, CarOnTheDrive.com) pick you up at the airport and take you to your vacation destination where your rental car is waiting for you. Of course, you pay extra for this.

Departure Time: When returning your car, unless absolutely necessary, don't opt for the car rental agency's expensive gas fill-up (unless they offer a free tank). And don't be stressed about getting to the agency at the exact time of return. Most places give you a couple of hours extra before they charge you for another day (though check your contract first).

DRIVING AN AUTOMATIC

Cars are usually automatic transmission. America has very few vehicles with manual gears [stick shifts]. Here are some tips for driving an automatic...

- When you turn on the ignition, you may need to wiggle the steering wheel a bit to release it.

- Automatics have six gear positions: P (Park), R (Reverse), N (Neutral), D (Drive), 1 (first gear) and 2 (second gear). You won't need to use the first or second gears in Central Florida, as these gears are for climbing steep hills and the landscape here is flat. Just drive in the normal driving position (D) and the gears will automatically change.

- If the gear lever is in a centre console, to release press the gear lever button first (on side or top of lever). With some vehicles, you need to apply the brake slightly to move the lever.

- Use only the right foot when driving an automatic, both for the accelerator [gas pedal] and the brake.

- Although easy to drive, it can be monotonous driving an automatic on lengthy trips. Never risk falling asleep driving on America's long, straight roads. If possible, take turns with another insured driver or take a break and stretch your legs or stop for coffee or even take a short nap at a safe Rest Area service spot.

- Remember that the steering wheel is on the left side of the car, but you'll be driving on the right-hand side of the road. Most lane mistakes are made when pulling out of petrol stations [gas stations] or shopping areas or when turning at traffic lights or when entering a traffic-free road and you forget what side you should be on.

- Don't forget to put the car in Park (P) before turning off the ignition.

WHAT TO EXPECT ON THE ROADS

In Florida, especially around theme parks, you're sharing the road with other inexperienced tourists and people who have moved here from out-of-state or another country, so you need to have patience. Americans may think nothing of driving long distances, but in Greater Orlando, for a variety of reasons, drivers have gotten into some bad habits such as weaving in and out of lanes without indicating or jumping red lights. However, the wide, straight roads can make driving a pleasure, especially if you avoid the rush-hour traffic, early morning and late afternoon.

Rush Hour: In some parts of Orlando – particularly along the I-4 Highway – congestion is an on-going problem, so try to avoid early morning and late afternoon rush-hour driving. (See also Motorway Driving on page 123.)

CULTURE SHOCK TIP

As a reminder to drive on the right-hand side of the road, wear your watch on your right-hand wrist.

Erratic Drivers: As mentioned before, drivers in Florida tend to weave in and out of lanes without warning and without using their indicators [turn signals]. There's nothing you can do except keep a sharp eye open and give room to drivers who cut you off. It's certainly not worth a confrontation with the other driver, as you never know how this could escalate.

Smoke: Due to forest fires in the dry season, smoke may cause difficult driving conditions. If you come across smoke, turn your low beams on as you would in fog, and drive slowly. To prevent wildfires during severe droughts, it's against the law to throw, drop or dispose of a match, cigarette or cigar out the car window.

Heavy Rain: By law, you must turn on your car headlights in the rain. Beware of slippery, oily road conditions. And at any time avoid driving or turning around in the grass ditches at the side of the road, as they can be swampy and you could get your tyres stuck.

CULTURE SHOCK TIP

Don't flash your headlights at another driver to signal you are letting them in, or for any other courtesy reason. Flashing your headlights at another driver in America often means WARNING.

Heat: Your car soon heats up like a furnace in the sun, so never leave children or pets unattended (even with the windows open). Also, watch out for hot seat-belt buckles that may burn skin. To keep the car cool, learn how to use the car's air-conditioning controls.

Parking: Be careful where you park your car. Don't park within 15 feet of a fire hydrant (see picture) or kerbs painted yellow. And don't park facing oncoming traffic.

Theft: Especially during the Christmas shopping period, don't leave valuables and packages on display in the car; lock them in the boot [trunk].

Traffic Signals: Lights do not have the amber-and-red together warning. They just have a red, amber, green, sequence. Watch out for vehicles illegally going through red lights (known as red-light runners). However, it is legal to turn right on a red light if it is clear to do so (see rules on next page).

TURNING RIGHT OR LEFT

When you're driving on the 'wrong' side of the road, turning left or right can be tricky. Statistics show vehicles turning (usually left) are a major cause of accidents, so below are some safety turning tips.

Turning Right: One great aspect to driving in America is, after coming to a complete stop first, you can turn right on a red traffic light [stoplight], if it is clear to go. Of course, there are exceptions – you must look out for NO RIGHT TURN ON RED signs at some junctions [intersections].

Turning Left: When turning left, remember to give way [yield] to oncoming traffic. Many roads have centre turning lanes used only for turning left. Don't forget to signal before entering these lanes.

Turning Left at Traffic Lights: When turning left at a traffic light, remember you are driving on the opposite side you're used to, so be careful not to accidentally end up facing oncoming traffic by driving to the wrong side of the road.

Watch Out!: When turning either left or right, motorists must by law give way to pedestrians and cyclists crossing the road.

Important! If you're going straight ahead in a multi-lane road, avoid the far right-hand lane or you'll annoy those trying to turn right on a red light.

CULTURE SHOCK TIP

Turning Right: You can turn right on a red traffic [stop] light if it is clear to go. (See rules above)

SPEED LIMITS AND POLICE PROCEDURES

Speed Limits: While driving, keep a lookout for speed limit signs, which are posted in miles per hour. Many main roads in Orlando have a speed limit of 55 mph (or 45 mph or less, depending how close to urban areas they are). The maximum allowable speed limit on some rural motorways [interstate highways] is 70 mph. The speed limit around residential areas is usually 30 mph or 25 mph, or less.

Important! Speeding fines are doubled close to road works when road workers are present. On the flip side, you can also be pulled over for driving too slow on motorways [interstate highways].

Breakdown and Accidents: Traffic police are helpful and will pull over to assist in times of breakdown or accident. The emergency number for police, fire and ambulance is 911. And if you have a mobile [cell] phone *FHP will connect you to the Florida Highway Patrol.

TIP Switch on your hazard lights if you are breaking down or driving in hazardous weather.

Don't Drink and Drive: The laws are severely enforced for drink driving crimes.

Important! You must store alcohol in the car boot [trunk] as it is an offence to carry it inside your vehicle.

Police: If the police, highway patrol state trooper or sheriff (yes, they still have sheriffs) want you to stop, they will flash their lights at you and may even turn on their siren for a second. They expect you to pull over, turn off your engine, and if it is night, reduce your headlights to parking light position. STAY IN YOUR CAR and wait for instructions – do not get out of your vehicle unless requested to do so, as this is considered an aggressive move. Most likely the police will want to see your driver's license and car hire [rental] agreement. Don't look for these until they ask you to, as they may think you are looking for a gun (no kidding). Keep your hands on the steering wheel, act politely and don't argue.

122

Buckle Up – It's The Law

- All front seat passengers must be buckled.

- Child-restraint seats are mandatory for children 3 years and under.

- Children ages 4 through 5 must be in a secured booster seat or a safety belt. The driver is responsible for buckling up the child.

Important! Safety studies show that when a child's seat belt doesn't come across the shoulder at the proper angle, then the child will slip out of the belt during an accident.

Street Smarts: According to several independent reports, metro Orlando is ranked one of the most dangerous places for pedestrians in the USA. Please be extra careful when crossing the road, especially at night when it's hard to judge traffic speed. Try to cross where there is a traffic light or centre island [raised median], and don't let your children run on ahead. Look both ways. Remember, the traffic is coming from a different side of the road to Britain.

MOTORWAY [Interstate/Freeway] DRIVING

On dual carriageways [multi-lane or divided highways] and motorway [Interstate or I roads], Floridians are notorious for hogging the outside or 'fast' lane while driving slowly. Don't be tempted to flash your lights or beep your horn at those who do – you'll be wasting your time and could add to possible road-rage situations. Offending motorists do this because exiting is both from the right- and left-hand side of the motorway [Interstate] and Americans choose the lane they are going to exit in a mile or two, just in case they can't move over in time. Therefore, there is no such thing as the 'fast' lane. Also, American drivers often just stick to the middle lane because they don't want to get caught when a lane suddenly becomes an exit. You'll never change this behaviour, so best just to accept it as part of the American driving experience.

TIP Vehicles overtake you on both sides of the highway, and this is perfectly legal. So watch out for vehicles on either side when moving into any lane.

Merging On and Off Lanes: An entry or exit slip road is known as an on- or off-ramp. There are usually no exit warning countdown signs, however, sometimes there is a mileage destination sign, such as: 24 miles to Exit 68. And information signs for hotels, motels, petrol [gas] and eateries are also posted prior to some exits. Certain lanes are marked: EXIT ONLY. If you don't want to exit, you must get out of this lane. But if you ever miss your exit turn-off, do not back up, as this is an extremely dangerous thing to do – just get off at the next exit – and don't worry, you'll be able to get back to the road you were travelling on (although this may be inconvenient, it's better than taking dangerous risks). And never, never stop in the road. If you are breaking down, pull over to the side verge [shoulder] safely.

PUDDLE ON THE ROAD

Don't panic if you see clear fluid on the ground spilled from under your car. It's only air-conditioning condensation and nothing to be concerned about.

Pumping Petrol [Gas/Gasoline]

- Petrol Stations are called Gas Stations and are all self-service (which is not so in some US states).

- Gas is measured in US gallons and prices are much lower than the UK (at least half the price).

- To pump petrol [gas] you must follow the on-screen instructions, such as choosing payment method and grade of gas.

- Sometimes to start the pump, you have to pull up the lever the petrol [gas] nozzle sits on.

TRAFFIC SIGNS

Below find explanations of some American road signs you may not have heard of . . .

PED XING stands for Pedestrian Crossing. America does not use animal names such as Zebra Crossing to indicate crossings. And don't always expect vehicles to halt when you are waiting at the kerbside of a non-lighted pedestrian crossing.

HAZMAT stands for Hazardous Materials (dangerous goods).

WRONG WAY means you are driving the wrong way on a slip road [ramp] exit. Or it means you are heading towards a one-way road. Do not enter and turn around safely immediately.

NO PARKING ON PAVEMENT means no parking on the road (does not mean sidewalk). Pavement in America stands for any paved area.

 YIELD means give way.

SCHOOL ZONE means you are driving near a school and must watch out for children. You must also observe the speed limit posted during times noted (see School Buses on page 127).

CENTER TURN is a sign indicating a lane for turning left (never overtake in this lane). Don't be alarmed if you see vehicles coming towards you from the other direction, drivers from either direction may use the centre lane (unless otherwise indicated).

 RAILROAD CROSSING is a sign for a railway track. You must never stop on this track even if you can't see a train coming.

Flashing Traffic Signals

If you come across a flashing traffic light . . .

- **Flashing Red:** Come to a complete stop; give way to all other traffic and to pedestrians. Proceed only when the way is clear.

- **Flashing Amber:** Many motorists think they have to stop at flashing amber lights. Don't unless there is a need to. Just slow down and proceed with caution.

How to Handle 4-Way or 3-Way Stops

 Roundabouts [traffic circles] in Florida are rare. Instead, find lots of traffic lights and thousands of **STOP** signs. Most are at junctions [main intersections] and many of them are 4-Way or 3-Way Stops where every car approaching the junction must come to a complete stop.

Here are the steps for 4-Way and 3-Way stop signs . . .

1. Come to a complete stop.

2. The driver who arrived at the junction first goes first. Then the driver who arrived second pulls out.

3. If two cars reach the junction at the same time, the driver on the left gives-way to the driver on the right.

4. If everybody arrives at the same time, try to make eye contact and look for the 'you-go-ahead' wave before plunging in.

Source: Orlando Sentinel newspaper.

Note: In America, you give way [yield] to traffic coming from the left at roundabouts [traffic circles].

SCHOOL BUSES

During school terms you may encounter the American iconic bright yellow school buses that transport children to and from school. Be alert and watch out for children who may dart from around these buses. There are certain important Florida laws of the road you must follow, which are detailed below, and you could be slapped with a fine for not following the rules.

TIP Police officers sometimes ride school buses to catch violating drivers of vehicles on the road who don't stop.

What To Do When a School Bus Stops

1. When a school bus stops and flashes red lights and its stop sign arm is extended out at the side, then the driver is stopping to let children on or off.

2. Traffic approaching from EITHER direction in ALL lanes must stop. You must stop in the opposite direction as well, even if there is a centre turning lane or painted lines in the middle of the road.

3. You cannot overtake the bus when it is coming to a stop or has stopped altogether.

4. You may not proceed again until all children are clear of the roadway and the bus lights stop flashing.

5. However, the rule for divided roads is somewhat different. (A left turning lane does not make the road a divided road.) A divided road is one that has a raised barrier or unpaved central reservation [median] at least five feet wide. On a divided road, only traffic going in the SAME direction as the bus is required to stop, but ALL lanes going in the same direction as the bus must still stop.

TOLLS

In America, road construction and maintenance is partially paid for by the revenue earned at tollbooths. Keep some quarters (25 cent coins) and dollar bills handy for these tolls.

TIP Tolls do not accept credit cards.*

CLASSIC CARS AT OLD TOWN
www.MyOldTownUSA.com

Vintage American cars can be spotted at Old Town (looks like an English fairground) on Highway 192 (Irlo Bronson Highway), Kissimmee. Check website for the nights of car shows and parades.

Lane Types: When approaching a toll you'll notice all tollbooth lane types are clearly marked: those that take coins only, those that give change, and those that are E-pass lanes.

E-Pass Lanes: Be sure you don't go through the E-pass (or Sunpass) lanes. These are designated for resident pass holders and you can't pay here with cash. If you do accidentally go through an E-pass lane, keep going, as it is dangerous to stop. However, to save time and hassle you can purchase an E-Pass transponder at Walgreens pharmacies and sign-up for a month as a tourist. Just renew and reload every time you come to Florida.

TIP Some tolls on exit roads charge less than a dollar and are unmanned, so always keep quarters (25c coins) handy for these in your car.

*Hertz car rental, however, offers the Platepass system. For a nominal rental fee all tolls are automatically paid as you drive through, and your credit card will be automatically charged.

NAVIGATION

Compass: For navigational purposes just remember to think in terms of north, south, east and west. For instance, someone may give you the following directions: 'Go north on Highway 417, then turn west on . . .' well, you get the picture. It's a good idea to bring a car compass or rent a Sat Nav [GPS] system with your vehicle.

TIP When asking for directions, remember to ask whether roads are going east, west, north or south bound or you could end up driving for miles in the wrong direction.

Road Names

You may find it handy to know that the main roads/highways around Orlando are . . .

- **Interstate 4** (I-4 for short). The main Interstate motorway [highway] through Orlando that starts in Tampa and ends in Daytona.

- **Irlo Bronson Memorial Highway** (US 192). Cuts east to west through Walt Disney World and Kissimmee.

- **Colonial Drive** (State Road 50). Cuts across the centre of Florida, east to west through Orlando, ending at Weeki Wachee. Its name is Colonial Drive in the section through Orange County.

- **Florida's Turnpike.** Major road running north to south Florida, crossing the I-4 in Orlando, and ending in Miami.

- **International Drive** (I-Drive for short). Winding road where many area attractions are situated (though not Disney World).

- **Orange Blossom Trail** or OBT (US 441). The US 441 is a north to south motorway [highway] 433 miles long from Miami to Georgia border. The Kissimmee section is known as Orange Blossom Trail.

- **John Young Parkway** (State Road 423). Is an alternate to Orange Blossom Trail that runs parallel.

- **Osceola Parkway** (County Road 522). Is a 12-mile, east-west road across Osceola County. Connects Disney World with Interstate 4 and Florida's Turnpike and ends at Boggy Creek Road near Buenaventura Lakes.

- **Beachline Expressway** (Toll 528). Road to Orlando International Airport, known as the Beachline because it leads to the Atlantic coastline and towns Cocoa Beach and Cape Canaveral.

- **Central Florida Greenway** (Toll 417). Road in east Orlando that begins and ends on the I-4.

- **Toll 429.** This highway serves as an entryway to Walt Disney World from northwest Orlando.

Directions: If you don't have a Sat Nav [GPS], go to Google Maps (https://Maps.Google.com) or Map Quest (MapQuest.com) to print out directions to and from your hotel, airport or any other destinations you require.

GOT YOUR LICENSE?

You can use your British driver's license in the US on holiday [vacation]. Keep it with you in the vehicle along with your hire [rental] car agreement.

DRIVING TERMS & TRANSLATIONS

BRITISH	AMERICAN
Bonnet	Hood
Boot	Trunk
Bumper	Fender
Camper Van	Conversion Van
Car Hire	Car Rental
Car Park	Parking Lot
Caravan	Trailer
Central Reservation	Median
Diversion	Detour
Dual Carriageway	Multi-lane Highway
Enter/Exit Slip Road	On-Ramp/Off-Ramp
Exhaust Pipe	Tailpipe
Flyover	Overpass
Give Way	Yield
Hand Brake	Emergency Brake
Indicators	Turn Signals (or Blinkers)
Junction	Intersection
Lay-by	Rest Area (or Rest Stop)
Lorry	Truck
Manual Gear	Standard/Stick Shift
Motorway	Interstate/Freeway
Multi-storey Car Park	Multi-level Parking Garage
Number Plate	License Plate (or Tag)
Pavement	Sidewalk
People Carrier	Minivan
Petrol	Gas/Gasoline
Petrol Station	Gas Station (or Service Station)
Ring Road	Beltway
Roundabout	Traffic Circle (or Rotary)
Taxi Rank	Taxi Stand
Toll Road	Turnpike
Van	Pick Up

BRITISH	AMERICAN
Verge	Hard Shoulder
Windscreen	Windshield
Zebra Crossing	Crosswalk
	(or Pedestrian Crossing)

9 OFF THE THEME PARK TRACK

W hen a change of pace is in order, away from the hectic theme parks, Florida has a wide variety of places to offer and things to do: Wildlife, nature, beaches, boating, dinner shows, golf, just to name a few. Most places in this chapter are local to the Greater Orlando area, though some are roughly an hour or two drive away.

DISCOVERING NATURE

FLORIDA STATE PARKS *Tel: 1-850-245-2157*

www.FloridaStateParks.org THROUGHOUT FLORIDA there are over 150 state parks. At 1.5 million acres, the Everglades, which starts at Kissimmee River and flows south for 100 miles, is Florida's largest park. For details on all Florida parks, go to website in the address above. For details of parks in the downtown city of Orlando, go to website: cityoforlando.net/fpr

FOREVER FLORIDA RANCH *Sat Nav Address: 4755 N. Kenansville Road, St. Cloud, 34773. Tel: 407-957-9794 or Reservations 1-866-85-4EVER. Location: Roughly thirty miles south of Orlando. www.ForeverFlorida.com* ZOOM OVER THE TREETOPS on an adventurous Zipline (maximum 68 feet off the ground) or experience a wildlife journey in an elevated Coach Safari vehicle. Or why not take a guided horseback trail through this 4,700-acre Forever Florida ranch.

BLUE SPRING PARK *Sat Nav Address: 2100 West French Avenue, Orange City, 32763. Tel: 1-386-775-3663. Location: Roughly one-hour drive north of Orlando (Arrive early to ensure admission) www.FloridaStateParks.org/Bluespring* AS YOU WALK THE WOODED TRAILS of Blue Spring Park, it's easy to imagine the Timucuan Native Americans living among the trees and canoeing the springs as they did for hundreds of years here. During November to March, peaceful manatees find haven in the warm spring waters. (For more manatee information, go to Wildlife Tips on page 191.)

Note: Check out SJRiverCruises.com for boat tours and cabin rentals at Blue Spring Park.

TIP In order to spot the manatees at Blue Spring Park, make sure you walk the full length of the boardwalk.

SILVER SPRINGS STATE PARK *Sat Nav Address: 5656 East Silver Springs Blvd., Silver Springs, 34488. Tel: 1-352-261-5840 (Mon-Fri). Location: SR 40, East of Ocala, off I-75, Exit 352 Roughly 90 miles from Orlando. www.SilverSprings.com* OPENED IN 1878, Silver Springs State Park covers 350 acres. A great place to view sparkling, crystal-clear pure waters in glass bottom boats, as well as the world's largest artesian spring, which is a spring that taps groundwater so that water rises without pumping.

WEKIWA SPRINGS STATE PARK *Sat Nav Address: 1800 Wekiwa Circle, Apopka, 32712. Tel: 407-884-2008. Location: Off I-4, Exit 94. www.FloridaStateParks.org/WekiwaSprings* NATURAL PARKLANDS – 7,800 acres – where you can canoe, hike and picnic. (Arrive by 10:30 AM on weekends and public holidays, as this park sometimes closes due to full capacity.)

WEEKI WACHEE SPRING *Sat Nav Address: 6131 Commercial Way, Spring Hill, 34606. Tel: 1-352-592-5656. Location: 100 miles west of Orlando. www.Floridastateparks.org/Weekiwachee* THIS UNUSUALLY NAMED SPRING ('Little Spring' in Muskogee Native American language) is one of the original tourist attractions of Florida. Here you'll find a water park, river cruise and underwater theatre 'mermaid' show (call for times of show).

TIP Go to PaddlingAdventures.com for canoe and kayaking tours at Weeki Wachee Spring. And for fancy afternoon tea in the area: Magnolia Terrace Tearoom (MagnoliaTerraceTeaRoom.com). For more information, go to Luxury Afternoon Tea on page 101.

BOK TOWER GARDENS *Sat Nav Address: 1151 Tower Blvd., Lake Wales, 33853. Tel: 1-863-676-1408, Tickets and Info: 1-863-734-1222. Location: Exit 55 off I-4, head South on U.S. Highway 27 (check website for detailed directions) www.BokTowerGardens.org* SET IN 245 ACRES of lush tropical gardens on the highest point of Lake Wales Ridge. The gardens have an unusual 205-foot high marble bell tower where you can hear clock music on the half hour.

HARRY P. LEU GARDENS *Sat Nav Address: 1920 North Forest Avenue, Orlando, 32803. Tel: 407-246-2620. Location: Downtown Orlando. www.LeuGardens.org* THESE TRANQUIL 50-acre tropical and sub-tropical gardens are famous for their colourful Azalea collection that blooms in spring (end of Feb/beginning of March). They also have many other plant collections, including Bamboo, Banana Tree, as well as a Butterfly Garden.

TIP Harry P. Leu Gardens has free entry on the first Monday of every month (check website above for details).

AIRBOAT RIDES

To experience Florida's wildlife – alligators, manatees, bald eagles, blue herons, otters, birds and turtles – why not take a guided tour on an airboat.

BIG TOHO AIRBOAT RIDES *Sat Nav Address: 2264 East Irlo Bronson Highway, Kissimmee, 34744 (office). Tel: 321-624-2398. Location(s): Rides on Lake Jackson or Kissimmee River State Park www.BigTohoAirboatRides.com*

BOGGY CREEK AIRBOAT RIDES *Sat Nav Address: 2001 E. Southport Road, Kissimmee, 34746. Tel: 407-344-9550, Toll Free: 1-877-304-3239. Location: Kissimmee chain of lakes. www.BCAirBoats.com*

BLACK HAMMOCK AIRBOAT RIDES *2356 Black Hammock Fish Camp Road, Oviedo, 32765. Tel: 407-365-1244 (also has a 'Call Me Skype' button on their website). Location: North East of Orlando. www.TheBlackHammock.com*

TIP Check to see if airboat operators provide proper ear protectors. If not, bring earplugs or noise cancelling headphones, as these boats are fun but noisy.

SPACE EXPLORATION

 National **A**eronautics and **S**pace **A**dministration

KENNEDY SPACE CENTER *[American spelling] Tel: 1-866-737-5235. Location: Off SR 405 (check website for full directions) www.KennedySpaceCenter.com* YOU'LL NEED TO schedule a full day to tour Kennedy Space Center for the bus tours, Imax films, and displays in order to discover everything from spacecrafts to moon rocks to the $100 million Space Shuttle, Atlantis.

Note: For area information call: Florida Space Coast Office of Tourism www.VisitSpaceCoast.com, Tel: 1-877-572-3224 or 321-433-4470.

TIP For good spots to witness awe-inspiring rocket launches: Either from the Kennedy Space Center special launch viewing areas or go to Port Canaveral Jetty Park, 400 Jetty Road, Cape Canaveral, 32920 www.JettyParkBeachAndCampground.com/park_index

PADDLEWHEEL BOAT CRUISES

INDIAN RIVER QUEEN *Tel: Toll Free: 1-800-979-3370 (or for Private Charters Tel: 1-321-454-7414). Boarding Location: Cocoa Village Marina, 90 Delannoy Avenue, Cocoa, 32922. www.IndianRiverQueen.com* BUFFET OR JUST SCENIC CRUISES on an old time glamorous, triple deck, paddlewheel boat in the Cocoa Beach area.

Note: For getting married on the Indian River Queen, see also Wedding Locations in MISCELLANEOUS TIPS chapter on page 199.

BEACHES

GULF COAST (FloridasBeach.com): The nearest beaches on the calm, warm Gulf coast waters in the west are Clearwater, Treasure Island, and St. Petersburg, roughly a two-hour drive away. These are all long, wide stretches of sand. It's unusual to find small coves in Florida, though this means you'll always find a good spot on the beach and parking close by.

TIP Fort DeSoto Park has an award-winning sugar-sand beach with numerous campsites for those that like to get away from it all. Tel: 1-727-582-2267, www.PinellasCounty.org/park/beaches.htm

HOLIDAY HOMES IN FLORIDA

www.DiscoverVacationHomes.com
(click Florida on the map)

ATLANTIC COAST: Roughly one-hour drive away, the nearest popular beaches to Orlando on the Atlantic Ocean are: Cocoa (CocoaBeach.com) a surf town in the so-called Space Coast area; New Smyrna (NSBFLA.com); and touristy Daytona Beach (DaytonaBeach.com) where you'll find designated areas on the beach for driving your car.

TIP Looking for an affordable guesthouse to stay in? Try searching BedAndBreakfast.com

Swimming Safety Tips

- Never swim alone.

- Never leave children unattended.

- Never swim in a thunderstorm or hurricane.

Undertows or undercurrents plague much of Florida's coastline. Stay in the areas with a lifeguard if possible. If you get caught in a rip current [rip tide] don't try to fight it. Swim to the side of the current until in safer waters, at which time you can swim ahead safely to shore.

Note: For tips on sunbathing, go to MISCELLANEOUS TIPS chapter on page 189.

INDOOR SURFING

FANTASY SURF *Sat Nav Address: 5151 Kyngs Heath Road, Kissimmee, 34746. Tel: 407-396-RIDE. Location: Fantasy World Resort, off Poinciana Boulevard between SR 535 and Highway 192 www.UltimateIndoorWave.com* CLIMATE CONTROLLED INDOOR surf pool. Learn to ride the wave on either a bodyboard (42 inch height minimum) or a smaller flowboard (52 inch height minimum). Beginners or experienced surfers welcome. The walls are padded for wipeouts.

Important! Fantasy Surf doesn't open until 3 PM throughout the week. Fri-Sun opens at 11 AM.

INDOOR SKY-DIVING

IFLY ORLANDO *Sat Nav Address: 6805 Visitors Circle, Orlando, 32819. Tel: 407-903-1150. Location: Off International Drive (I-Drive) www.iFlyOrlando.com* NO JUMPING from an airplane required for this exhilarating flying simulation, and no previous experience necessary. The vertical wind tunnel has fans that reach speeds of 120 mph acceleration, which is the speed required to keep you afloat.

HOT AIR BALLOONS

 ORLANDO BALLOON FLIGHTS *(merging Orange Blossom Balloons and Blue Water Balloons) Tel: 407-786-7473. www.OrlandoBalloonFlights.com* OFFERS SUNRISE balloon flights, seven days a week, weather permitting. flights followed by buffet breakfast.

THOMPSON AIRE BALLOON RIDES *Tel: 407-421-9322*

www.ThompsonAire.com SUNRISE FLIGHTS near Disney World. (See also Wedding Locations on page 199.)

TIP If don't have a car to drive to the meeting points, for an extra fee, hotel pick-ups are available at both balloon-ride companies detailed above.

RACING CAR EXPERIENCES

WALT DISNEY WORLD SPEEDWAY EXOTIC DRIVING EXPERIENCE *Sat Nav Address: 3450 N. World Drive, Lake Buena Vista, 32830. Tel: 407-939-0130 or Toll Free: 1-855-822-0149. Location: Walt Disney World, just beyond Magic Kingdom parking toll plaza. www.ExoticDriving.com/race-track/orlando-walt-disney-world-speedway* GET BEHIND THE WHEEL of a racing Ferrari, Lamborghini or Porsche and take the one-mile lap.

DAYTONA INTERNATIONAL SPEEDWAY *Sat Nav Address: 1801 W. International Speedway Blvd., Daytona Beach, 32114. Tel: 1-800-PITSHOP (call or go online for schedule of races) Location: Off I-95 on US Route 92; adjacent to Daytona Beach Airport. www.DaytonaInternationalSpeedway.com*
DAYTONA HOLDS the famous races of NASCAR, Automobile Racing Club of America, American Motorcyclist Association, and Motorcross. For fanatics there's the Sprint FANZONE pit area (ticket prices depend on race). Here you can inspect the garages, inspection bays and drivers' crews.

ZOOS, ETC.

CENTRAL FLORIDA ZOOLOGICAL PARK & BOTANICAL GARDENS (AND ZOOM-AIR ADVENTURES)

Sat Nav Address: 3755 N.W. Highway 17-92, Sanford, 32771
Tel: 407-855-5496. Location: Highway 17-92 at I-4, Exit 104
www.CentralFloridaZoo.org CENTRAL FLORIDA ZOO has 400
animals to view and a zipline aerial adventure (extra charge) to ride on. For
summer fun you'll find splash fountains at the front of the park, so perhaps
pack your kiddie's swimsuit and flip-flops or swim shoes. You can bring
your own picnic to the outside picnic tables, though coolers are not allowed
inside the zoo.

GATORLAND *Sat Nav Address: 14501 S. Orange Blossom Trail,*
Orlando, 32837. Tel: 407-855-5496 or Toll Free: 1-800-393-5297
Location: Off Highway 441 (between Orlando and Kissimmee)
www.Gatorland.com ONE OF ORLANDO'S original tourist attractions,
featuring alligators up close and personal with shows, demonstrations and
gator wrestling. There's also cute furry animals for interactive encounters,
and a Screamin' Gator Zipline for overhead views of lush gardens filled
with crocs and, of course, alligators.

GREEN MEADOWS PETTING FARM *Sat Nav Address: 1368*
South Poinciana Blvd., Kissimmee, 34746. Tel: 407-846-0770
Location: Five miles south of Highway 192, Kissimmee
www.GreenMeadowsFarm.com ENJOY A CHARMING, quiet day
discovering three-hundred cute animals. You'll also find tours and hayrides.

BREVARD ZOO *Sat Nav Address: 8225 North Wickham Road,*
Melbourne, 32940. Tel: 1-321-254-9453. Location: Off I-95, east of
Exit 191 (roughly one-hour's drive from Orlando) www.BrevardZoo.com
BUILT BY LOCAL volunteers, Brevard Zoo is the only zoo in the US to
offer kayaking tours. Other activities you'll find: Tree-top Trek Aerial
Adventures; a ten-minute Train Tour; and a self-guided Paddleboat ride.

TIP Hand-feeding the giraffes at Brevard Zoo at the Expedition Africa exhibit is
a once-in-a-lifetime experience, if you're lucky enough to be there when the
giraffes approach the elevated feeding platform (usually in the morning).

CIRCUS WITHOUT ANIMALS

CIRQUE DU SOLEIL *Sat Nav Address: Buena Vista Drive, Lake Buena Vista, 32830. Tel: 407-939-7328. Location: Disney Springs, off I-4 or off Highway 192. www.CirqueDuSoleil.com* PART CIRCUS (NO ANIMALS), part acrobatics, part Broadway show. Worth the Broadway ticket prices too. Note: There's also a different Cirque Du Soleil show at the Amway Center [American spelling] at 400 West Church Street, Orlando, 32801. Tel: 407-440-7000, AmwayCenter/events.com

HORSE RIDING

HORSE WORLD RIDING STABLES *Sat Nav Address: 3705 Poinciana Blvd., Kissimmee, 34758. Tel: 407-847-4343 www.HorseWorldStables.com* SITUATED ON 750 ACRES in the Kissimmee countryside, a place to enjoy organised nature trail rides for all levels of horse riding [horseback riding] experience, seven days a week.

TIP Disney horse riding: https://disneyworld.disney.go.com/recreation/tri-circle-d-ranch

AIRCRAFT MUSEUM

FANTASY OF FLIGHT museum is now closed except for private hires.

A FLYING AND WORKING MUSEUM

WARBIRD ADVENTURES INC. *Sat Nav Address: 233 North Hoagland Blvd., Kissimmee, 34741. Tel: 407-870-7366 or Toll Free: 1-800-386-1595. Location: Kissimmee Gateway Airport www.WarBirdAdventures.com* WHEN HOLLYWOOD needs real warplanes they come knocking on Warbird Adventures' doors. Available for everyone else: Flights aboard World War II trainer planes.

TITANIC

TITANIC THE EXHIBITION *Sat Nav*
Address: 7324 International Drive, Orlando 32819
Tel: 407-248-1166. Location: Close to Universal
Studios www.TitanicTheExperience.com/orlando
PERMANENT TITANIC attraction with guided tours, artefacts, and full-scale replicas. You'll really feel you're on the ship. (See also in this chapter: Titanic Dinner Adventure in Dinner Shows section on page 145.)

TIP At the Titanic museum, bring along something warm to slip on for the cold room areas.

HANDS-ON SCIENCE

ORLANDO SCIENCE CENTER [American spelling]
Sat Nav Address: 777 East Princeton Street, Orlando, 32803.
Tel: 407-514-2000 or Toll Free: 1-888-OSC-4FUN. Location:
North of downtown Orlando. www.OSC.org
HANDS-ON SCIENCE EXHIBITS for children and adults. OSC also has the world's largest cinedome, which screens nature and adventure films daily.

ALL-AMERICAN TOWN

CELEBRATION *Location: Off Highway 192 (next to Old Town)*
http://CelebrationTownCenter.com/events
CELEBRATION IS AN AWARD-WINNING Disney-designed village. Stroll along tree-lined streets and view picturesque homes with porches, shutters and picket fences. The central village has shopping, dining and special events such as 'snow-fall' at Christmas and a pie festival in May.

Celebration is the best place to be at Halloween

SPANISH HISTORICAL TOWN

ST. AUGUSTINE *Location: 104 miles northeast of Orlando; less than a two-hour drive from Orlando. www.OldCity.com* WHO SAYS AMERICA has no history? Founded in 1565, this Spanish town with its sea-front fort is the oldest and most charming city in Florida. There's a whole street of original buildings where you can watch artisans create their wares. You can also visit the oldest wooden schoolhouse in America.

TIP The King's Head British pub. Sat Nav Address: 6460 U.S. Highway 1 North, St Augustine, 32095. Tel: 1-904-823-9787 (call first for hours).

GREEK HISTORICAL TOWN

TARPON SPRINGS *Location: Off I-4 heading towards Tampa; two and a half hours from Orlando. www.SpongeDocks.net* IF ST. AUGUSTINE is a Spanish town, then Tarpon Springs is a Greek one. Here you'll find Greek shops, a marina, sponge boats, and the highest ratio of Greek immigrants in the US. Tarpon Springs historical routes are connected to the sponge-diving industry. Now it's just a nice place to watch a gulf-coast sunset or enjoy a plate of Moussaka in one of the many Greek restaurants.

DINNER SHOWS

MEDIEVAL TIMES DINNER AND TOURNAMENT
Sat Nav Address: 4510 W. Vine Street, Kissimmee, 34746. Tel: 1-866-543-9657. Location: Off 4510 W. Irlo Bronson Hwy., Kissimmee. www.medievaltimes.com/orlando.aspx THIS SHOW FEATURES jousting battles and knights on horseback. Don't miss a tour of the on-site eleventh century Medieval Village.

PIRATES DINNER ADVENTURE *Sat Nav Address: 6400 Carrier Drive, Orlando, 32819. Tel: 407-248-0590 or Toll Free: 1-800-866-2469. Location: Off International Drive www.PiratesDinnerAdventure.com/Orlando* SWASHBUCKLING MUSICAL and aerial stunt production aboard a full-scale replica pirate ship.

SLEUTH'S MYSTERY DINNER SHOWS *Sat Nav Address: 8267 International Drive, Orlando, 32819. Tel: 407-363-1985 or Toll Free: 1-800-393-1985. Location: Off Universal Blvd. www.Sleuths.com* FEATURING AUDIENCE interaction, murder-mystery comedy shows.

TITANIC DINNER ADVENTURE *Sat Nav Address: 7324 International Drive Orlando, 32819. Tel: 407-248-1166. Location: Titanic The Experience Museum www.TitanicTheExperience.com/Orlando/special-events/titanic-dinner-event.html*

DINE WITH THE FAMOUS passengers of the Titanic: Featuring survivor Molly Brown, ship's designer Thomas Andrews, Captain Smith and others. See the Grand Staircase, and watch the bridge as the captain and officers encounter J. Bruce Ismay, Chairman of shipping company White Star Line. The cast walk freely throughout the room during the meal and mingle with guests.

CAPONE'S DINNER & SHOW *Sat Nav Address: 4740 W. Irlo Bronson Highway, Kissimmee, 34746. Toll Free: 1-800-220-8428 Location: Off Highway 192. www.AlCapones.com*

STAND-UP COMEDY AND MUSICAL productions with audience interaction, all set in the 1930's Al Capone era. Dinner is a buffet that includes drinks.

DISNEY'S SPIRIT OF ALOHA DINNER SHOW

Sat Nav Address: 1600 Seven Seas Drive, Lake Buena Vista, 32830 Tel: 407-WDW-DINE (939-3463). Location: Disney's Polynesian Village Resort (on the Magic Kingdom monorail route) www.DisneyWorld.disney.go.com

POPULAR FAMILY-FRIENDLY, all-you-can-eat, South Pacific dinner and show, featuring hula dancing and a fire-knife performer. This show is open air so check if closed due to stormy weather.

AMERICAN SPORTS

ESPN WIDE WORLD OF SPORTS *Sat Nav Address: 700 South Victory Way, Kissimmee, 34747. Tel: 407-939-1500. Location: Off I-4, Exit 65. www.espnwwos.com* EXPERIENCE AMERICAN SPORTS – baseball, basketball, softball, tennis and American football – all at clean, modern stadiums in a family atmosphere.

DISNEY HOTELS CLOSE TO WIDE WORLD OF SPORTS
Disney's Pop Century Resort
Disney's Art of Animation Resort

AMWAY CENTER [American spelling] *Sat Nav Address: 400 West Church Street, Suite 200, Orlando, 32801. Tel: 407-440-7000 Location: Downtown Orlando. www.AmwayCenter.com* HOME OF ORLANDO MAGIC basketball team, Solar Bears ice hockey team, and Orlando Predators American football team.

ORLANDO CITY SOCCER CLUB

Major League Soccer (MLS) club opening a
US$155 million new stadium (2016) with a
crowd capacity of 25,500
www.OrlandoCitySC.com

Meanwhile, this team play at the Citrus Bowl
www.OrlandoCitrusBowl.com

GOLF CLUBS

Florida is known as the golfing capital of America. The beauty of golf here is the year-round warm weather, so you can play nearly every day. Below is an alphabetical list of some clubs open to tourists.

ANNIKA ACADEMY *Sat Nav Address: 7450 Sparking Court, Reunion, 34747. Tel: 407-662-4653 or Toll Free: 1-888-266-4522 Location: Reunion Resort, Kissimmee. www.TheAnnikaAcademy.com*

CELEBRATION GOLF *Sat Nav Address: 701 Golf Park Drive, Celebration, 34747. Tel: 407-566-4653. Location: The Disney-built town of Celebration. www.CelebrationGolf.com*

CHAMPIONS GATE GOLF CLUB *Sat Nav Address: 1400 Masters Boulevard, Champions Gate, 33896. Tel: 407-787-4653 Location: Next to the Omni Resort, Exit 58 on the I-4, Kissimmee www.ChampionsGateGolf.com*

 DISNEY WORLD GOLF Disney has four golf courses, three with the same address at: *Sat Nav Address: 1950 West Magnolia Palm Drive, Lake Buena Vista, 32830. Tel: 407-WDW-GOLF (939-4653) Location: Disney's Grand Floridian Resort, Magic Kingdom* :

1. Disney's Magnolia Golf Course
https://disneyworld.disney.go.com/recreation/magnolia-golf-course

2. Disney's Oak Trail Golf Course
https://disneyworld.disney.go.com/recreation/oak-trail-golf-course

3. Disney's Palm Golf Course
https://disneyworld.disney.go.com/recreation/palm-golf-course

4. Disney's Lake Buena Vista Golf Club *Sat Nav Address: 2200 Golf Drive, Lake Buena Vista, 32830. Tel: 407-WDW-GOLF (939-4653), Disney Springs.*
https://disneyworld.disney.go.com/recreation/lake-buena-vista-golf-course

TIP Disney's sports and recreation: https://Disneyworld.disney.go.com/recreation

FALCON'S FIRE GOLF CLUB (MARRIOTT'S) *Sat Nav Address: 3200 Seralago Boulevard, Kissimmee, 34746. Tel: 407-239-5445. Location: Off W. Osceola Parkway. www.FalconsFire.com*

GRANDE PINES GOLF CLUB (MARRIOTT'S) *Sat Nav Address: 6351 International Golf Club Road, Orlando, 32821. Tel: 407-239-6108. Location: Close to SeaWorld. www.Marriott.com*

HAWK'S LANDING GOLF CLUB (MARRIOTT'S) *Sat Nav Address: 8701 World Center Drive, Orlando, 32821. US Toll Free: 1-800-567-2623. Location: Orlando World Center Marriott Resort, Lake Buena Vista. www.GolfHawksLanding.com*

HUNTER'S CREEK GOLF CLUB *Sat Nav Address: 14401 Sports Club Way, Orlando, 32837. Tel: 407-240-4653. Location: Close to Florida Mall. www.GolfHuntersCreek.com*

SHINGLE CREEK GOLF CLUB *Sat Nav Address: 9939 Universal Boulevard, Orlando, 32819. Tel: 407-996-9933 or Toll Free: 1-866-996-9933. Location: At the Rosen Shingle Creek Hotel; close to International Drive. www.ShingleCreekGolf.com*

MINIATURE GOLF

Miniature golf in Florida is fun and usually good value for money. Courses often have themes such as alligators or pirates.

 Pirate's Cove has three miniature golf courses and Pirate's Island has one:

PIRATE'S COVE

Pirate's Cove Lake Buena Vista *Sat Nav Address: 12545 State Rd. 535, Orlando, 32836. Tel: 407-827-1242. Open year round www.PiratesCove.net*

Pirate's Cove Orlando *Sat Nav Address: 8501 International Drive, Orlando, 32819. Tel: 407-352-7378. Open year round. www.PiratesCove.net*

Pirate's Cove Kissimmee *Sat Nav Address: 2845 Florida Plaza Blvd., Kissimmee, 34746. Tel: 407-396-7484 (call for seasonal hours) http://www.piratesislandgolf.com/kissimmee-fl-pirates-cove*

PIRATE'S ISLAND *Sat Nav Address: 4330 W. Vine Street, Kissimmee, 32746. Tel: 407-396-4660 www.PiratesIslandGolf.com/kissimmee-fl-pirates-island (call for seasonal hours)*

 Disney has two miniature golf courses:

DISNEY'S FANTASIA GARDENS *Tel: 407-560-4870. Location: Across from Disney's Hollywood Studios. www.DisneyWorld.disney.go.com* Theme based on the movie Fantasia.

DISNEY'S WINTER SUMMERLAND *Tel: 407-560-4870. Location: Adjacent to Disney's Blizzard Beach water park. www.DisneyWorld.disney.go.com* Both winter/Christmas and summer/seaside themes.

Universal has two miniature golf courses (18 or 36 holes) at the same location:

UNIVERSAL STUDIOS MINIATURE GOLF *Tel: 407-802-4848. Location: Next to Universal Cineplex at Universal CityWalk. www.HollywoodDriveinGolf.com* Hollywood Drive-In Golf. Theme: 1950's horror/sci-fi movies, complete with fun special effects.

10 THE ARTS

I t's a surprising fact to many, but there's plenty of culture and arts in the land of the mouse. Everything from museums to ballet to art; even a Philharmonic Orchestra.

TIP Before visiting museums and theatres, always telephone first for opening hours, admission charges (including details of any special family packages), directions or, if needed, whether there are any restaurants or cafes on site or close by.

BROADWAY IN ORLANDO *Sat Nav Address: Dr Phillips Performing Arts Center, 455 S. Magnolia Ave, Orlando, 32801 Tel: 407-423-9999 or Toll Free: 1-800-448-6322 http://Orlando.Broadway.com* ENJOY AWARD-WINNING BROADWAY productions. In the past they've staged Chicago, War Horse, and Mama Mia.

CHARLES HOSMER MORSE MUSEUM OF AMERICAN ART *Sat Nav Address: 445 North Park Avenue, Winter Park, 32789 Tel: 407-645-5311 (closed Mondays and major holidays) www.MorseMuseum.org* LOCATED IN the established tree-lined town of Winter Park, the Morse Museum of American Art is a showcase for authentic Tiffany glass, including a chapel, jewellery, pottery, paintings and, of course, their famous lamps.

CULTURE SHOCK TIP

'I'm going to WILL CALL to pick up the tickets'

WILL CALL is a ticket booth where people who have purchased their theatre or concert tickets (on the phone or over the Internet) can pick them up. Usually situated next to the box office.

CORNELL FINE ARTS MUSEUM *Sat Nav Address: 1000 Holt Avenue, Winter Park, 32789. Tel: 407-646-2526 (closed Mondays and major holidays and for installations of new art exhibits) www.rollins.edu/cfam* ALSO LOCATED IN WINTER PARK, this art museum is in the lush grounds of Rollins College, overlooking the lake.

MAD COW THEATRE *Sat Nav Address: 54 West Church Street, Second Floor, Orlando, 32801. Tel: 407-297-8788 www.MadCowTheatre.com* AWARD-WINNING, professional theatre company. Everything from Chekhov to Pinter.

ORLANDO MUSEUM OF ART *Sat Nav Address: 2416 N. Mills Avenue, Orlando, 32803. Tel: 407-896-4231 (closed Mondays and major holidays) www.OMART.org* THIS MUSEUM PRESENTS exhibitions of local, regional, national and international significance. Exhibits include early and contemporary permanent collections of American art, as well as ancient Americas and African art collections.

SHAKESPEARE FESTIVAL at Lowndes Shakespeare Center *Sat Nav Address: 812 E. Rollins Street, Orlando, 32803. Tel: 407-447-1700* *Located in the Loch Haven Cultural Park. Season: September-May www.OrlandoShakes.org* PRODUCES SHAKESPEARE CLASSICS as well as contemporary productions.

ORLANDO BALLET *Sat Nav Address: 2211 N. Orange Ave, Orlando, 32803. Box Office Tel: 407-426-1733. Season: October-May plus Christmas when classical ballet The Nutcracker is performed. www.OrlandoBallet.org* INTERNATIONAL MIX of gifted dancers, showcasing world-class performances, held at the Bob Carr Performing Arts Centre in downtown Orlando (or at the new Dr Phillips Center for the Performing Arts).

ORLANDO PHILHARMONIC ORCHESTRA *Sat Nav Address: 812 East Rollins Street, Suite 300, Orlando, 32803. Tel: 407-896-6700. Box Office Tel: 407-770-0071, www.OrlandoPhil.org* THE PHILHARMONIC'S eighty musicians perform everything from Beethoven to Broadway. More than one-hundred performances a season. Go to website to check their schedule.

WINTER PARK SIDEWALK ARTS FESTIVAL *Location: Central Park, along Park Avenue in town of Winter Park www.WPSAF.org* SINCE 1960, this outdoor art festival has been held every year for one week during March. Displaying hundreds of pieces from artists, sculptors, jewellery-makers and photographers, both American and international.

ENZIAN THEATER [American spelling] *(Art House and Independent Films). Sat Nav Address: 1300 South Orlando Avenue, Maitland, 32751. Tel: 407-629-1088 (or for listings Tel: 407-629-0054). Location: Close to Winter Park (see website for directions) www.Enzian.org*

With an audience appreciation you won't find in mainstream cinemas, the Enzian is a special place for art house and independent film lovers. Choose from chez-lounge, comfy-chair or table seating. Meals and wine served at your table or chair during the film! The Enzian is also home to the annual Florida Film Festival.

TIP Due to high demand for film tickets at the Enzian, reservations are usually recommended.

CULTURE SHOCK TIP

In America, the term theatre (sometimes ending in er, sometimes re) can mean either a traditional theatre or a movie theatre.

11 PROPERTY PURCHASE TIPS

A fter first falling in love with Florida on holiday [vacation], you may decide to invest in a holiday home or even try to move here permanently. This chapter outlines the buying process and the possible pitfalls. It also explains the types of visas, including immigration and non-immigration. And, if you're thinking of moving to the Sunshine state, there's some helpful advice coping with culture shock.

TIP For peace of mind, always work with professionals – lawyers, estate agents [realtors], house appraisers – preferably those experienced in assisting British buyers through the US process.

BUYING A HOLIDAY HOME

If you wish to purchase a property in Florida, there are no restrictions on foreign ownership. But before you start the home-buying process, it is advisable to do your homework first.

The first thing to consider is the housing market. When the recession hit Greater Orlando, property halved in value compared to the boom of 2000-2006, however, since 2013, prices have steadily increased. Bargains are still to be had, though don't rely on holiday [vacation] rental income to pay for your mortgage. Think long-term investment or second home.

Also, in this economic climate it's unadvisable to invest in a property not yet built (called buying off-plan). Too many builders have gone bankrupt and many Brits have lost their deposits or life savings in the process.

However, in the last few years, properties in short-term let [rental] holiday resorts have sold out to British buyers. The town of Davenport in Lake County is particularly popular, although not as close to Disney as Kissimmee is. There have been whole housing estates [sub-divisions] built for the sole purpose of selling to overseas buyers. But for rental income generated from these homes, the nearer the location to Walt Disney World, the higher the value.

TIP Kissimmee is much closer to Walt Disney World than the downtown City of Orlando is.

PROPERTY WEBSITES

Two search sites when looking for US homes online:
www.Trulia.com
www.Realtor.com

Compare Prices: British homebuyers receive far more for their converted pound when buying in Florida compared to Britain. Such as the opportunity to buy spacious, open-planned homes with several bedrooms, two+ bathrooms, air conditioning and a swimming pool. Beware of property companies who sometimes inflate house prices to overseas buyers who are comparing the prices to back home. Check online for the comparative prices for homes in the neighbourhood you're thinking of buying in. Search for the actual price homes sold for. Since the property bubble burst, reductions in the offer price of between $4,000 up to $25,000 have been accepted.

TIP When searching on a property website, in the search preferences section, click 'single-family home' for sale, which is a house or villa for a family.

HANDY WEBSITE
www.BritishFlorida.com

The above website is the F.A.B.B.
(Florida Association of British
Businesses) with advice to give to British
house buyers as well as those interested
in purchasing businesses for a visa to live
in America.
(Go to: Non-Immigrant E2 Business Visa
on page 167 for more information.)

Next to consider is quality. Many houses look fine cosmetically, and prospective buyers can be wowed by extra features offered – ensuite bathrooms, screened-in pools, open kitchens complete with over-sized appliances – but don't get stars in your eyes with options that are standard in Florida. In other words, don't jump at the first place you view. It's also a good idea to research the builder's reputation, especially the type that constructs huge estates.

Remember, also, if you're buying a new build, that the show [model] home is fitted with every possible extra feature, and if you want these add-ons they're going to considerably increase the base price.

TIP When house hunting, try to ignore decor – furniture, colour of paint, window treatments, carpets, etc. – these are all aspects of the house that can easily be improved to your taste.

Avoid Problems: When you find a property you like, stroll around the neighbourhood and ask the residents some questions about living in the area and the standard of building work, etc. Be prepared to walk away if things don't sit right. Some houses are fine until the first hurricane hits. There've been horror stories of houses with water pouring through unsealed walls, as well as into the gaps of poorly fitted windows. Then, when the humidity hits, damp and mould grows out of control. The insurance company won't pay. The builder won't pay. Owners are stuck with a mortgage or their life savings gone.

TIP Keep in touch with the local news for building articles, such as newspaper site: OrlandoSentinal.com. Another handy site to check for consumer alerts is MyFloridaLegal.com (this is the Attorney General of Florida website).

Travel Visas: As a Brit, you're entitled to be in the US for three months of the year under the ESTA visa waiver programme (See: Passports, Visa Waivers & ESTA in KNOW BEFORE YOU GO chapter on page 173). Or you can apply for a B2 Visa issued for 10 years that lets you stay for up to six months at a time. To apply for a B2 Visa, you will need: a valid passport with a validity date of at least six months beyond your intended stay; evidence of sufficient funds to live on; and evidence of homeownership in your own country and/or employment ties. (It is easier to obtain if you are retired). Be aware that, on average, 25% of British B2 applicants are denied, which also makes you unlikely to get ESTA approval for about six months in order to travel on the Visa Waiver programme!

TYPES OF PROPERTY SALES

- **Open Market:** A straightforward sale.

- **Bank Owned:** Foreclosure. Owners have lost the house to the bank.

- **Short Sale:** The owners can't afford to pay their mortgage and are trying to sell before foreclosure. Their bank or mortgage company has to approve the buyer's offered price. Process can take 6 months to years to close.

- **Auction:** Usually held at the county courts of the home's location. Buyers can bid on properties and possibly snag a bargain. It's a good idea to inspect beforehand.

Rental Income: Many estate agents [realtors], property brokers and property management companies have set up shop in the area specifically to cater to overseas purchasers. Brokers may promise that the return on rental income will pay for your mortgage. More than likely, if you're expecting the rental income to cover the mortgage, repairs, house taxes, and other management fees in their entirety, you will probably be disappointed. Often, there will be weeks in the year when the house is empty, especially November to March. See Short-term Rental and Long-term Rental under Property Terms & Translations on page 164.

Important! If you're looking to rent out your house to holidaymakers when you're absent, you must purchase a property in a community zoned for short-term rental.

TIP Take digital photographs of any home features you like. At the end of a long day of house hunting, looking through these will help in the decision-making process.

Loans & Mortgages: There are several types of mortgages for the British buyer, with lenders who offer varied interest rates. Only go to an established and reputable lender who has a reputation you can verify. Then make sure you lock in your interest rate and find out from the lender how long you can lock in that rate for. **Get it in writing.** Ask about any fees that the lender charges. Beware of hidden fees. Ask for the Annual Percentage Rate or APR of the loan. This is the actual cost of the yearly mortgage. To save disappointment, try to get pre-approval on a mortgage before house hunting. This is different from pre-qualification, which is just a brief analysis of your finances and not a guarantee of mortgage.

STEPS TO BUYING A PROPERTY

Below are the basic steps for purchasing a property in Florida. If you're paying cash for your investment, the whole process to closing can take as little as 10 days. With a mortgage it takes roughly 3-6 weeks. Your closing can be 'mail away' if you're signing back home in Britain, where documents can be sent by email or fax. You may need a notary in the UK when signing. Also, at certain dates during the whole process, different documents need to be signed. **Important!** You risk losing your deposit and the seller backing out of the house sale if you miss any document signing dates.

TIP You may find it useful to know that in America, when a date is numerically written, the month always comes first. So 8th April 2014 or 08/04/2014 would be written 04/08/2014.

1. Find an Agent
Estate Agents are called Realtors or Real Estate Agents or Brokers. They must be licensed and have professional qualifications. There are two types in Florida: The agent for the buyer, and the agent who represents the seller (don't tell seller agents any confidential information, such as the highest price you're willing to buy for).

You need only one buyer's real estate agent, since in America all agents have access to the MLS (Multiple Listing Service) database of properties for sale, so you don't have to go from agent to agent in order to view different properties. The agents are happy because the seller's agent splits their commission with the buyer's agent. You're happy because you don't have to pay an agent for their services, which often includes being driven around to show you different properties and help in the buying process.*

TIP When discussing your list of preferences to realtors, say 'check list' not 'tick list'.

2. Open a Foreign Currency or Foreign Exchange Account

It's a good idea to open a Foreign Exchange bank account that will save you money when transferring UK funds. You can use either a British bank or the services of an exchange company like Smart Currency Exchange (SmartCurrencyExchange.com).

3. Find a Real Estate Attorney

It's advisable to have a real estate attorney look over the PURCHASE CONTRACT before you sign it.

Important! Once signed, you can't easily back out. It's a good idea to make your purchase subject to one or any of the following contingency protections:

a) **Mortgage/Loan Contingency:** Don't forget to include the amount and, most important, the interest rate.

b) **Home Inspection Contingency:** (or the seller making necessary repairs after inspection). Homes in Florida are also inspected for termite infestations by a licenced inspector. Termites eat wood from the inside out and can destroy a home.

c) **Sale Contingency:** If the home purchase depends on you selling your property.

d) **Appraisal Contingency:** If you want to, you can have an independent appraisal carried out in order to find out the market value of the property.

TIP Have your attorney word any of the above contingencies.

*Due to possible conflict of interests, Florida law now limits estate agents [realtors] from offering dual (both buyer and seller) representation.

4. Make an Offer

Once you've found the house you like, make an offer through your realtor. This offer will then be accepted, rejected or counter-offered. When the property offer has been accepted, you will sign a binding purchase contract (see No. 3 above) and pay a small goodwill deposit (not to be confused with the down payment) to a third party such as an estate agent [realtor] or Title company. Obtain a receipt.

5. Make a Deposit (Mortgage Down Payment)

Usually for foreign investors, from 20% to 35%. The deposit should be placed in an Escrow attorney account for your protection, and will be released on house closing.

6. Extra Expense

Don't forget to factor into your home-buying costs: Legal fees, taxes, closing fees, searches, loan fees, inspection fee, mortgage insurance, title insurance, stamp duty, which all tag on an approximate 5% to 6% of purchase price. As well, account for yearly expenses: property tax, tax on rental income, private medical insurance or travel insurance, cost of rental management company fees if you're letting your home to holidaymakers [vacationers], home insurance, repairs and maintenance, utility bills (gas, electric, water), and Homeowners Association (HOA) fees (see Property Terms & Translations below).

7. Home Inspection

Don't skip this step. For the amount of around $300 you could be protected from buying a home with major defects. If, after inspection, repairs are needed, you should inform the seller. If you've accounted for a contingency in your contract (see: Find a Real Estate Attorney, No. 3 above), you can either renegotiate your contract or have the seller make good on any repairs.

8. Title Search

The next step is a title search. A Title Company searches the history of the house and finds out whether the property is free and clear of mortgages, taxes or liens (see: Title Insurance in Property Terms & Translations below).

PROPERTY TERMS & TRANSLATIONS

Here's an alphabetical list of the common real-estate language you'll come across in Florida in pursuit of your American dream…

Condo: Short for Condominium. This is an apartment where you own the inside, but a Homeowners Association (HOA) owns everything outside. Homeowners share the cost of maintenance and other fees. Not recommended, as many issues arise from owning a condo, particularly for overseas buyers.

Escrow: Transferring or exchanging money/property using a neutral third party.

For Sale by Owner: Property not represented by an estate agent [realtor]. You'll still need a real estate attorney.

Foreign National Finance: A mortgage or loan for non-US citizens that requires at least 30% deposit (difficult to obtain for new builds).

HOA: Homeowners Association. Every housing estate [sub-division or community] has a homeowners association and each homeowner must pay an annual fee to pay for the upkeep of any communal pools, playgrounds, tennis courts, clubhouse and common lawns, etc. The HOA must also approve for short-term rental of the homes in their community.

Important! If you don't pay your Homeowners Association fees, HOA's can foreclose on your property.

MLS: Multiple Listing Service. A computer database of property for sale that all estate agents [realtors] have access to.

Mother-in-law Apartment: Granny Flat.

Proof of Funds: A letter or recent statement from your bank to show you can pay for the property with cash.

Property Management Company (or Rental Management Company): A company who looks after your home and find tenants or vacationers for it. Usually, they recommend or offer services such as house cleaning companies, pool cleaning, lawn [yard] maintenance, furniture and appliance stores, plumbers, etc. It's important to find a reliable management company, especially as you'll be thousands of miles away from your property. And don't forget to factor in their charges in your yearly budget.

TIP To find a property management company on the Internet, Google: **Vacation Property Management** Orlando or Kissimmee (or the area you're buying in).

Pre-Approval Letter: A letter from your finance or mortgage company to show you can finance the property. (As mentioned, this is different to pre-qualification, which is just a brief analysis of your finances and not a guarantee of a mortgage).

Realtor: Estate Agent.

Short-term and Long-term Rental: If you're in the market for a vacation investment property, make sure that the estate [sub-division] is zoned for the short-term rental market and that the sub-division's Home Owners Association rules approve it. You can then rent it out to holidaymakers [vacationers] for less than seven months of the year. Long-term Rental: Allows you to rent to tenants for longer than 7-month leases, usually in one-year leases. Don't buy in a long-term rental only area if you want to use your home for renting out to holidaymakers [vacationers].

Note: Short-term Rentals: You must also apply for a Tourist Tax License and a Business License if you are not using a Management Company who will usually do this on your behalf.

Sub-Division: Another name for housing estate.

Title Insurance: To protect the buyer from any future issues to do with liens (loans or mortgages) on the property. The insurance is a one-time only payment. The Title Company searches county records for the buyer.

Tourist Development Tax (nickname: Bed Tax): Tax that is charged by the government on holiday rentals. Counties charge between 5%-6%. Your property management company will usually collect for you.

TIP Orlando is in Orange County. Kissimmee is in Osceola County. Haines City and Davenport are in Polk County. Clermont is in Lake County.

Townhouses: A row of attached, multi-floor houses (similar to terraced houses, though in Florida usually modern).

Zone: Each area of land is divided into zones. There are four main types: residential, commercial, agricultural and industrial. Your house or apartment will be in a residential zone. (See Short-term and Long-term Rental above for further details).

THINKING OF MOVING TO ORLANDO?

Immigration & Employment: You don't have to emigrate to America in order to invest in a property. However, if you want to be an immigrant or work here on a non-immigrant visa it is advisable to consult an immigration lawyer because the laws are complicated and frequently change, and the backlog of certain immigration applications can sometimes be years. This section explains the different ways to enter the US, and once you're here, strategies to deal with culture shock.

TIP Currently there are no retirement schemes for foreigners to the US. But retirees can buy a holiday home.

What's a Green Card?: A green card is a permanent residency card for immigrants to the US.

- Green Card holders can work but must pay taxes on their worldwide income, the same as US citizens.

- Green Card holders cannot vote.

- Green Card holders can apply to become US citizens (Brits do not lose their UK Passport but gain dual nationality) after 5 years (or 3 years if married to a US citizen).

TIP To speed the process for applying for citizenship after having a Green Card, submit your application at 4 years and 9 months (or 2 years and 9 months if married to a US citizen).

Qualifying: To obtain a Green Card in the United States, you must qualify for one of the following . . .

- Be sponsored by a US citizen who is a relative (spouse, sibling, child or parent) and who has enough income to support you.

- Be sponsored by a US legal permanent resident (spouse or parent) who again, has enough income to support you.

- Be Northern Irish and enter the yearly Diversity Visa Green Card Lottery (not available to other UK citizens). Beware of online scams. The US government will never write to you via the Internet or ask you to send money via Western Union or any other money-sending service.

- Have a US employer apply for a Labour Certificate for you and then file an Immigrant Petition. Visas are for persons of extraordinary ability: professors, researchers, skilled workers, and also for unskilled workers or artists, athletes, information technology specialists, agricultural workers, investors, nurses, broadcasters and ministers of religion.

- Invest in a business in the Immigrant Investor Programme in the amount of $1,000,000 or $500,000 if in a rural area or one of high unemployment, which will create at least 10 new full-time jobs for US citizens (an EB-5 Visa).

Note: For further information on Green Cards and Employment or Business Visas, go to US Government website: www.uscis.gov

HANDY WEBSITE

For Forums, Blogs & General Information

www.BritishExpats.com

The Non-Immigrant E2 Business Visa: Another way to move to the US is to run a business that employs Americans. These immigrant businesses inject more than $775 billion into the US economy. British citizens residing in the UK with a substantial sum of money (usually more than $50,000) to invest in a company can move to Florida on a non-immigrant E2 Visa, and many do. (It doesn't lead to a permanent Green Card but it does give you a Social Security number). Beware of scams. If you're looking for the American dream, don't let it become a nightmare. Hire a proper immigration lawyer/consultant experienced in the process, and check facts first.

Important! Under current law, holders of E2 business visas may reside in the US only until their visas expire (they are renewable but must be renewed in person at a US embassy in the UK every few years) or if the business fails or if they retire. Children of visa holders must leave the country when they reach age 21 if they haven't got their own E2 investment visas, citizenship, student status visa, or work as an E2 manager. If your children are school age or under, then age 21 may seem a long way off. But heart-breaking stories of families trying desperately to keep their children in the only country they can remember are common. So think long and hard if taking this route when you have children, or until the law changes.

TIP Spouses of E2 Visas have the right to legally work outside the business if they want to.

COPING WITH CULTURE SHOCK

Rollercoaster Emotions: You've made it to America and are living in the sun. You can't imagine having culture shock because you're so happy with your achievement. But culture shock can happen to anyone when thrust into an unfamiliar place with others who don't have the same way of doing things. Their customs may be different, as well as their habits, beliefs and behaviour. Studies tell us culture shock can make us feel ill, stressed, annoyed, angry, sad, disorientated, or even act withdrawn. It is normal and can happen to anyone who moves to a new country.

In the Beginning: At first, though, you'll probably be in what psychologists call the 'honeymoon period'. You're gazing at this new place through rose-coloured glasses and everything looks and feels wonderful. That period can wear off when the realities of life set in. Especially the first year when you have to sort out housing, schooling, employment, vehicles, as well as the everyday routines of grocery shopping, driving, after-school activities and/or day care. On top of that is the task of finding the right hairdresser, doctor and dentist, and if you have pets, a vet and maybe a dog walker or doggie day care. Just moving your pets over is a major job. You have to find the right airline, obtain the right dog or cat inoculations, health certificates, buy the correct pet carrier.

The British Way: The way we are, how we react to situations, are instilled in us from childhood. We British are usually a good natured and tolerant people. It's not in our nature to make a fuss; we patiently queue when others are pushing and shoving. We'll put up with not enjoying something rather than complain. Though anthropologists who study the British say we all enjoy a good moan – it's just that we do it in private.

Why Leave?: People go back to Britain from Florida for a variety of reasons: Inability to pay for healthcare insurance, homesickness, business or job failing, children's school issues, cost of universities, sick relatives back home, missing friends or family. Though, it's sometimes the little things that make people want to go home. Or a combination of little things. Because it's our day-to-day life that counts. It's like going to a restaurant where you love the food, but leaving early because the waiter upset you or your chair was uncomfortable or the lighting was too bright. In the end, you just couldn't enjoy the food, no matter how good it was.

The Little Things We Miss From Britain: Marks and Spencer, British TV, best back bacon, real Cadbury's chocolate, the countryside, the castles and history, football, Sunday lunch at the local pub, the sense of humour, a tiny fishing village or small cove, a favourite walk or a favourite city. Even the weather.

TIP You can have British foods delivered to your door in Orlando from: TheBritishShoppe.com or JollyGrub.com or BritishCornerShop.co.uk. And you can watch British TV shows already shown on iPlayers by hooking up your computer to your TV (or watching on your computer or tablet) and signing up with a system like SmartyDNS.com

Stiff Upper Lip: But there's nothing like the English resolve when things aren't quite going our way. That's why you'll overhear things like, 'We're not letting a spot of rain spoil our day out,' when a hurricane is approaching. Not to mention how our sense of humour defuses stressful situations. And how you handle where you're moving to depends on where you've come from. In other words, if you are improving your life in your new country, or have the prospects to, then you can appreciate things and cope better with life's ups and downs.

Surviving: Reading this book and learning the things you're going to encounter is a good start in helping you reduce culture shock. Giving yourself a break and taking things a bit slower, is another way. In other words, give yourself time to adjust. Don't catch the first flight out when things don't seem to be going your way. You'll regret it. If you're really homesick, take an extended trip back home, especially in the winter. After a couple of weeks enjoying the things you miss in Britain, you may find reality sets in and you are missing your new home back in Florida and the reasons you emigrated in the first place: the sunny weather, the standard of living, the opportunities, the quality of life, and not least, the friendly Americans who admire and welcome you.

Good luck.

12 KNOW BEFORE YOU GO

T his chapter covers everything from packing to flying to travel cash, because being prepared will cut down on stress levels and place you in a relaxed holiday frame of mind.

Note: For deciding on when to beat the theme park crowds, go to: BUSIEST TIMES OF YEAR on page 40. For advice on health insurance, go to: HEALTH TRAVEL INSURANCE on page 192.

TIP If dialling a UK telephone number from America, add the country code 011-44, and then drop the first zero of the phone number (if there is one) or you won't get through. For Ireland, the code is: 011-353.

AIRLINE TIPS

Airline	US Number	UK Number	Website
American Airlines	1-800-433-7300	0844-499-7300	AA.com
British Airways	1-800-AIRWAYS	0844-493-0787	BritishAirways.com
United Airlines	1-800-525-0280	0845-607-6760	United.com
Delta/KLM	1-800-241-4141	0871-2211-222	Delta.com
US Airways	1-800-428-4322	0845-600-3300	USAirways.com
Virgin Atlantic	1-800-862-8621	0844-209-7777	Virgin-Atlantic.com

TIP Flights are usually cheapest in January, February, September and October.

Finding Airline Deals: Booking flights online at websites such as LastMinute.com can save you money, though here's a surprising tip: Booking directly with the airline can be cheaper than booking with online companies such as: Ebookers.com, Expedia.co.uk, Edreams.com, SkyScanner.net, Kayak.co.uk, or Travelocity.com. By all means, check these aggregators first, then call the airline or go on their website to compare. (See more money-saving tips on the next page.)

Note: Don't forget to check if airline prices posted include all charges and taxes and whether your flight can be changed and/or cancelled.

Other possible ways of saving money on flights:

- Try to book your flight on a Tuesday (after 3 PM) when most airline sales kick in.
- If you can, book a flight after school holidays have finished. Avoid major holidays, too.
- Choose a night flight.
- Choose off-season.
- Try booking a flight online after midnight when flights are often cheaper.
- When on the phone, don't forget to ask the airline or tour company about any special sales or offers they may have, because they don't always tell you about these up front.
- Book flights either well in advance or last minute. Airlines like to fill seats at any price.
- Online flights that include hotels often cost less.
- Consider a package deal.

Note: See also Flying Tips on page 177.

PACKAGE TOURS TO ORLANDO

First Choice	FirstChoice.co.uk
Virgin Holidays	VirginHolidays.co.uk
Thomas Cook Signature	Tcsignature.com
Thomson	Thomson.co.uk
Travel City Direct	TravelCityDirect.com
British Airways Holidays	BritishAirways.com/Orlando

PASSPORTS, VISA WAIVERS & ESTA

British visitors can stay in the US for 90 days or less (you must have a return flight booked or they won't let you in). Your passport must be valid for at least 90 days from the date you enter the US, so check the date of expiration. And since April 2016, it must be a biometric (or e-passport).

UK PASSPORT OFFICE
National Adviceline
www.UKPA.gov.uk
Tel: (0)870-521-0410, open 24-hours, 7 days a week

US VISA EMBASSY
www.USembassy.org.uk
Tel: (0)9055-444-546

Important! ESTA: To travel to the United States you must sign-up for the Electronic System Travel Authorisation, known as ESTA, which allows you to travel under the Visa Waiver Programme. This replaces the old Visa Waiver green form you used to fill out on the plane. Your ESTA number lasts for two years or until your passport expires. You must fill out the ESTA form online at: https://esta.cbp.dhs.gov/esta

PACKING YOUR SUITCASE

TIP Too many British tourists shiver inside Florida's super chilly air-conditioned shops, restaurants, hotels and cinemas, so it's a good idea to always carry a cardigan or sweat top in case you need to cover-up.

What to Pack: Even in a Floridian winter you won't need a heavy coat – just jacket and jumpers [sweaters] and long trousers [pants] for the occasional cool day or evening. Don't forget to pack: sun hats or baseball caps, sunglasses and sunblock. Or purchase them in Orlando. It's essential to protect children and babies from the heat. Please remember a sun hat for baby. Avoid a trip to hospital A&E [called ER or Emergency Room] due to sunstroke. Hats with flaps to protect the neck are also a great option for children.

Luggage: If you're planning on some serious shopping, consider taking an empty holdall bag for the return journey. One of those fold-up types you can fit inside a suitcase will do the trick. Or, if you have children (not infants), take advantage of one of their airline luggage allowances and bring along an extra empty suitcase on wheels. But as outlined later in the SHOPPING TIPS chapter, be aware of excess baggage charges. Check with your airline for details.

Also check with the airline what size and weight of suitcase you're allowed. One of the best things you can in invest in is a set of portable/travel luggage weighing scales, especially handy for preparing for return flights after you've been shopping.

TIP To prevent someone taking your luggage by mistake (it does happen), you can make generic black suitcases stand out on the airport carousel by tying a strand of colourful fabric or ribbon around one of the handles.

Airport Security: Many people like to lock their suitcases, but if you do they may be pried open by Customs Inspectors. Either leave your luggage unlocked or use a TSA (Transportation Security Administration) approved lock, available for sale at most airports.

TIP Don't pre-wrap Christmas and birthday gifts because they can be torn open by Customs Inspectors.

Items Allowed: Airport security will allow pies and cakes through, but they are subject to screening. They won't let you bring in meat, seeds, fruit and plants. But you can pack inside your checked suitcase the following unopened items . . .

Items Allowed Inside Your Checked-In Suitcase

Cologne

Creamy dips and spreads

Gravy

Maple syrup

Jams and jellies

Perfume, lotions

Sauces, oils, vinegars

Salad dressing, soups

Wine, spirits [liquor], beer

Tea bags

Note: For security and safety reasons, some potentially dangerous items have been banned from being brought on planes. Check the latest prohibited items at the US government website (tsa.gov) for transportation security.

TIP Pack toiletries in see-through, plastic toiletry or freezer bags. Not only will these make your items visible to Customs Inspectors but also they will protect your luggage from any leakages.

Security Procedures: When you reach airport security, an immigration official will check your passport and take your digital photograph and finger scans. Never make security jokes with US Customs personnel. They won't find them funny, and you could find yourself being banned from the flight. Also, don't use your mobile phone, laptop, snap photographs, or do anything that may look suspicious to immigration personnel while you are in the security area.

TIP You must have any laptops or electronic devices charged-up and turned on, so that airport security can check that they're real.

 ## LEAVING YOUR HOUSE

Postpone: Don't forget to postpone the post [mail], newspapers and other deliveries.

Tour: Before you set off for the airport, take a last-minute tour of your home to see you haven't left anything on. However, if it's winter, leave heating on minimum to prevent freezing, ensuring you don't come back to burst pipes and a flooded home. Make the handy list that's on the next page, and stick it to your front door, then check you've everything with you on the way out to the airport.

Front Door List

Tickets/Boarding Passes
Passports and ESTA Number
Airline/Tour Operator Telephone Number
Wallet with Credit Cards
Cash/Traveller's Cheques/Travel Money Card
Travel Insurance Details
Driver's License
Car Hire Agreements
Hotel Confirmation Number
Previously Purchased Theme Park Tickets

FLYING TIPS

Orlando Has Two Main Airports:
ORLANDO INTERNATIONAL
www.OrlandoAirports.net

SANFORD AIRPORT
www.OrlandoSanfordAirport.com

Approximate Flight Times from London:
Orlando Airport: 9 hrs.
Sanford Airport: 10 hrs.

TIP Bulkhead or exit seats are the ones with extra legroom. But only people old enough to operate the emergency exit door can sit by the window here.

Delays: Flight delays and last-minute flight cancellations happen. In case of cancellations, bring your airline telephone number (or travel agent or tour operator telephone number) to the airport in order to reschedule without the inconvenience of waiting in long queues [lines]. When calling, ask the airline politely if you are entitled to free meals or a hotel night for a long delay, as compensation. Airline staff deal with a lot of irate passengers, so asking nicely goes a long way.

Checking In: To cut down on your own stress levels, allow plenty of time for checking in at the airport. Or to speed things up, check in online at home (from 24-hours beforehand) and choose your seats and print out your boarding passes to take with you. If you fly with Virgin Atlantic and are going from Gatwick, you can utilise their 'Twilight Check-in' for checking your suitcases the night before, leaving the day you fly that much less stressful (available between 5-9 PM at London Gatwick's South Terminal, Zone A).

What to Wear: For long-haul flights – and London to Orlando is at least nine hours – it's a good idea to wear comfortable travelling clothes. Avoid belts, buckles and jewellery that may set off sensitive metal detectors. Easily removable slip-on shoes are also convenient for going through security.

Have a Good Flight: Orlando is on US Eastern Standard Time Zone – that's five hours behind the United Kingdom*, which means you'll lose five hours sleep on your first night in Florida. Try to sleep on the plane, though I know this can be difficult with a cabin full of holidaymakers and children excited about Mickey Mouse. Take along a set of earplugs or headphones (especially useful are the noise-cancelling type) and eye mask to help you rest (see also Jet Lag Tips on next page).

So you won't be disturbed by the flight attendant telling you to fasten your seatbelt, wear it over your blanket. Don't sleep the whole flight, though. Air travel can cause deep vein thrombosis (blood clots) in the body, so you'll need to stretch your legs periodically to prevent this.

Drink plenty of water on the flight to stay hydrated and be aware that alcohol at high altitude has increased potency.

*Except when America changes daylight saving time two weeks before the UK, then it's six hours behind.

Flying with Children: Allow for plenty of toilet breaks and try to keep to feeding and sleeping schedules. Remove shoes of children who kick; the passengers in the seat in front will thank you. Better yet, don't allow your children to kick. Often they don't even realise that someone is sitting in front of them. Babies and tiny tots tend to cry on planes and toddlers sometimes don't want to be strapped down in their seat. Distract them with a soft toy. If they are old enough to understand, tell them what to expect on an aeroplane [airplane] beforehand and that they need to keep safe.

TIP To reduce ear pain from air pressure on takeoff and landings, let babies suck on a bottle of water or milk, and maybe give older toddlers a lollypop [sucker] to suck on.

Airport Taxi TIP: Don't accept rides from private car owners who try to solicit you and then may overcharge. Go to the official Orlando Airport taxi stand where the drivers have meters. Or use a pre-paid car service such as Quick Transportation (QuickTransportation.com).

Note: For more airport advice, go to: Airport Security on page 175.

Jet Lag Tips

- Upon arrival, immediately change your watch to Orlando time.

- Go to sleep at night in complete darkness. Light sends a message to the brain telling it to wake up.

- Avoid stimulants such as caffeine and alcohol.

- If you can manage to hold back eager children, go to theme parks when you feel rested.

US DUTY FREE ALLOWANCES

Bringing into the United States: You are allowed to bring up to $100 worth of new goods/gifts duty free. If the value exceeds $100, you will be required to pay duty. Those aged twenty-one and over can bring into the US: 200 cigarettes or 100 cigars and one litre of alcohol – beer, wine or liquor. As mentioned previously, don't bring in any meats, seeds, fruits and plants. You may bring in up to $10,000 in currency, but larger amounts must be declared to Customs (there's no limit on traveller's cheques).

UK DUTY FREE ALLOWANCES

Taking home to the United Kingdom: According to hmrc.gov.uk, on your return home you may import into the UK:

Alcohol: You can bring in either but not both of the following:

- One litre of spirits or strong liqueurs over 22 per cent volume.

- Two litres of fortified wine (such as port or sherry), sparkling wine or any other alcoholic drink that's less than 22 per cent volume.

In addition, you may also bring back both of the following: 16 litres of beer and 4 litres of still wine.

Or you can combine these allowances. For example, if you bring in one litre of fortified wine (half your full allowance) you can also bring in half a litre of spirits (half your full allowance). This would make up your full allowance. You can't go over your total alcohol allowance.

Tobacco: You can bring in ONE from the following list:

- 200 cigarettes
- 100 cigarillos
- 50 cigars
- 250g of tobacco

Or you can combine these allowances. For example, if you bring in 100 cigarettes (half your full allowance) you can also bring in 25 cigars (half your full allowance). This would make up your full tobacco allowance. You can't go over your total tobacco allowance.

Other Goods: You can bring in other goods worth up to £390 without having to pay tax and/or duty. Any goods over and above these allowances will be subject to duty. The amount of duty varies, depending on the type of item.

Banned Items: You CANNOT bring any meat or dairy products into the UK. For a full up-to-date list of other banned items, go to website: hmrc.gov.uk/customs/banned-restricted

TRAVEL MONEY

Every few yards, you find yourself stopping to buy high-priced theme-park food, theme-park merchandise, theme-park clothing and theme-park photographs of yourself looking theme-park ugly. Sometimes you stop and just spontaneously throw money into the theme-park air. You can't help yourself! You're theme-park stupid!

Dave Barry, Humour Columnist, discussing his yearly family trip to Orlando.

Money-Saving Tips

Despite the best-laid plans, unexpected expenses can ruin your budget, so here are a few money-saving ideas...

- When you're balancing your budget, you may like to know that theme parks charge more than average for drinks, ice creams, popcorn, camera film, batteries and sun oil, though sometimes buying these items is unavoidable.

- Watch out for unexpected expenses such as long taxi rides: ask for an approximate charge at time of booking, because Greater Orlando covers a lot of ground. For example, the distance from Disney World to Universal is approximately ten miles and can take anywhere from fifteen minutes to an hour, depending on traffic.

- Because portion sizes are so big in America (we're not kidding, you could feed an army on a family meal here), you can save money by sharing starters [appetizers] and desserts.

- Water is usually served free at the table in restaurants, unless you specifically ask for bottled. (For more eating out advice, go to DINING OUT TIPS chapter on page 85.)

Exchange Rate: At time of writing, the exchange rate for 1 GB pound is just over 1.69 US dollars, as posted at www.TheMoneyConverter.com.

Currency: Wherever you buy your USD currency, whether it's the bank, the post office, a cash exchange company, or a travel agency, ask about all the charges, such as exchange rates, commissions, handling fees, etc. Avoid airports to change your money as they often have the worst rates of exchange.

TIP MyTravelMoney.co.uk is a handy website comparing different rates for US Dollar travel cash and travel money cards.

Travellers Cheques: If you prefer to carry travellers cheques, you'll need to show your identification [ID] to cash them. Don't try to cash a $100 travellers cheque for some sweets [candy] or a sandwich; have smaller denomination ones handy. And have dollar notes [bills] for tipping and incidentals.

Using Credit/Debit Cards: To avoid carrying travellers cheques or large sums of money, you can use your UK bank credit/debit card to withdraw US money as needed from cash machines/ATMs. However, most banks charge a transaction fee every time you use a cash machine abroad, so don't make multiple small amount withdrawals.

- Check with your bank all their fees for foreign withdrawal and ask if they have an American corresponding bank relationship that saves you money on cash-machine fees.

- So you won't get short of cash on any given day, also check with your bank what your foreign DAILY cash-machine withdrawal limit per card is. You may need to increase it.

Important! You'll need a credit/debit card to reserve tickets for shows. And, if you try to book a car once you hit US soil, some car hire [rental] firms prefer a credit card instead of a debit card.

TIP At the cash register, your signature may be required if your PIN number is not valid in the US, in which case you will often be asked for photo ID such as a passport or driver's license.

TRAVEL MONEY CARDS

Pre-paid Cards: Another travel money option is pre-paid, reloadable travel money cards in USD currency. These include, among others: Virgin Money, Thompson and Thomas Cook (Cash Passport), and can be a safer and more convenient option than carrying wads of cash or travellers cheques. The advantage of these cards is you can keep your holiday [vacation] money separate from your bank account. And, if you lose or have this card stolen, no one has access to your bank account. For tips on which are the best and worst cards to use, go to website: MoneySavingExpert.com.

Important! Travel money cards are NOT good for booking your hotel or car hire [rental] as you don't want to have expensive holds put on them that tie up your cash.

TIP When paying your hotel or other bills with your debit/credit card, if asked what currency you would like to pay your bill in – dollars or pounds – always choose dollars to save on conversion rates and fees. Go to website: MoneySavingExpert.com for more advice.

Make a Note: If you lose your wallet, not only is it devastating losing the cash but also it's time-consuming cancelling all your debit/credit cards. To save hassle if your wallet gets lost or stolen, and to prevent fraud and identity theft, you should make a list of wallet/purse contents so you can cancel or renew everything quickly. Keep this list safe and, obviously, not in your wallet or in the bag where you keep your wallet.

Important Numbers List

Telephone numbers to report lost or stolen credit/debit cards

Passport number (or a digital photo of the passport's photograph page)

Health Insurance details

Driver's License number

BANKS

Banks in Orlando keep similar hours to banks in the UK. Most have open counters where the tellers are not hidden behind glass.

Drive Through: Some banks have drive-up facilities where, unlike inside banks, the teller is behind a glass window. If there are multiple drive-up posts, you park next to one and send your travellers cheques or card, along with your identification such as passport, up a pneumatic tube, after first talking to the teller through a speaker. The teller sends your money back down the tube to you. They are fun to use and kids get a kick out of them.

CULTURE SHOCK TIP
American Money Slang

Nickel	5 cents
Dime	10 cents
Quarter	25 cents
Buck	$1

TIP For emergency cash in minutes, you can have money sent to you via a Western Union office (WesternUnion.com).

 Bank at Disney: The bank for Walt Disney World is the SunTrust Bank on Buena Vista Drive, located just past Disney Springs going east. They offer basic services to non-account holders, such as cashing travellers cheques, credit card cash advances, wiring funds, etc. Note: Their cash machines are drive-up. *Address: SunTrust Bank, Lake Buena Vista Branch, 1675 Buena Vista Drive, Lake Buena Vista, 32830. Tel: 407-762-4786 or 1-800-786-8787.* **BANK HOURS:** *Monday, Tuesday, Wednesday, Friday 9:00 AM-4:00 PM. Thursday 9:00 AM-5:30 PM.* **DRIVE-UP HOURS:** *Monday, Tuesday, Wednesday, Friday 8:00 AM-5:00 PM. Thursday 8:00 AM-5:30 PM. Bank closed Saturday and Sunday.*

CASH FOR TIPPING

Tipping is in the Culture: There are places in the world where tipping is frowned upon – Japan – and places where tips are not expected to be substantial – Europe – but America is not one of them (hey, don't shoot me, I'm just the messenger). In return, the standard of service is high. You won't be left in a restaurant wondering when someone is going to offer you the dessert menu. You won't be faced with a frowning waiter when you ask for anything out of the ordinary. And it may help to remember that so much is often free in Orlando: coffee refills, children in hotel rooms, children's hotel breakfasts, Internet access, shopping car parks [parking lots], nature reserves, just to name a few.

But the subject of tipping in the States seems to generate a great deal of stress. It has to be said, Brits have a reputation for being poor tippers (maybe because we sometimes don't realize when to tip). Restaurant workers, maids and hospitality staff account for 64 percent of all minimum-wage earners. Is that your fault? No. But tipping is a small price to pay for everything Orlando has to offer, so it helps to be prepared. If you haven't already purchased American dollars in Britain, as soon as you exit your flight, obtain some small denomination notes [bills] for tipping. That way, you won't be worried about giving away your larger notes [bills]. But remember, $1 is not as valuable as £1.

Tipping Guide

Restaurants: 15%-20% tip is customary. Look over your restaurant bill [check] first, though, to see if you've been automatically charged a gratuity before inadvertently tipping twice.

Bars: $1-$2. It's customary to leave a tip, either when you pay for each drink or, alternatively, you can leave your tip on the bar on your way out.

Room Service: Don't forget to tip your room service waiter 10%-15%, but check first to see if a gratuity has already been added. You can also add the tip to your room by signing for it.

Bags: Airport Porters [Skycap], Hotel Porters and Bellhops usually get $2, or more if you have lots of luggage.

Doormen: $1 for hailing a cab and opening the door for you. Give extra if doorman helps with luggage.

Valet Parking: Attendants commonly get $2-$3 per car. Pay when you pick up your car.

Taxis: Taxi drivers typically are given a 15%-20% tip.

Concierge or Guest Services Desk: Under normal circumstances no tip is expected. But it's a nice idea to tip when you've been given a special service, such as for making difficult to find theatre/concert tickets, or for dinner reservations outside the hotel.

Housekeeping: Being a hotel maid is the hardest, lowest-paid and most under-appreciated job in a hotel, so tipping is really appreciated. Remember, the maid can't keep the tip if it isn't marked for her attention, so write on a piece of paper or envelope 'for housekeeping". Be generous if your room has been extra messy, however, $2-$3 per night, per room is the norm. It's also a good idea to tip each day to allow for maid shift changes.

Hairdressers: 15%-20% for hair stylists and $2-$3 for hair washers. (Keep the tip ready in your pocket so you don't have to go looking for the hair washer or stylist later.)

Spa: 15% of total cost if gratuity not already added to bill.

Golf Caddy: $20.

PLACES YOU DON'T NEED TO TIP: Supermarkets (even if someone loads your car); fast-food restaurants; self-service eateries (but do tip a couple of dollars at all-you-can-eat buffet restaurants if you've been served drinks); coffee shops; and any Disney transport.

13 MISCELLANEOUS TIPS

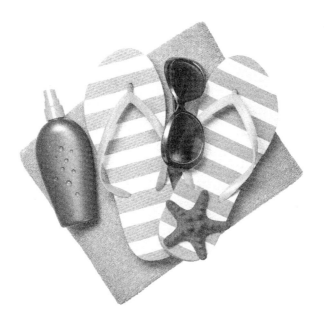

S o what's left to tell you about? Well, a miss-mash of topics with useful and important information for making your stay in Orlando successful, such as advice on where to find walk-in health clinics, what's going on with the weather, wildlife, and tips on making telephone calls, mailing letters and parcels – even a few wedding venue suggestions.

WEATHER TIPS

The weather, a favourite topic for us Brits, is usually warm year-round in Florida. When you look outside your air-conditioned hotel room, don't be fooled by the look of the sky on a cloudy day. Step out into the air and you'll realise it's probably warm. In fact, it's one of the joys of staying in Orlando – walking outdoors to be enveloped in warm air.

Winter: Florida in the winter can be warm. Though the months December to March often have cooler days, with lows of 9°C (49°F) and highs of 24°C (76°F). One day it can be cold and the next hot, so bringing layers is recommended.

Spring: April is nice and mild with temperatures ranging from 16°-29°C (61°-84°F).

Summer: During the warmer months – May to September – daytime temperatures range from 21°-32°C (70°-90°F) although with the humidity they can feel a lot hotter.

Autumn: The autumn [fall] months are extremely pleasant with temperatures 23°-28°C [mid-70's to mid-80'sF].

Rain and Thunderstorms: You won't hear this from tourism adverts, but during July to September Central Florida is prone to afternoon summer rainstorms due to the mix of cooler air coming from the coast, colliding with the warm inland air. If this is mixed with a lightning storm, don't take shelter under a tree or sit on any metal outdoors. Also, get out of the swimming pool and off the golf course, and avoid using a landline telephone. If you are driving in a rainstorm, either slow down with headlights on or, if visibility is poor, pull off the road altogether with hazard lights flashing. Usually, rain showers dissipate quickly (though they can be torrential) so just look for a temporary shelter until they pass. But it's a good idea to carry a plastic raincoat/poncho in your bag.

Weather Updates: While in Florida, you can get weather updates from the radio, the weather channel, as well as local news TV channels or from the local newspaper the Orlando Sentinel or at OrlandoSentinel.com/weather or Weather.com or by dialling Tel: 321-255-0212 (ext. 412).

Hurricanes: Hurricane season is June 1 to November 30, but being inland, Central Florida is usually protected. When hurricanes do hit the area, most tourist hotels and all the theme parks are usually up and running within the next day or two (unlike most of Florida, theme parks have their power lines underground for protection). Those staying in holiday [vacation] homes are sometimes without power for a few days, which can be a great cause of inconvenience. You should telephone your airport/airline or tour operator to check for any delays caused by a hurricane.

Important! Universal hotels have a 'No Questions Asked' cancellation policy if you can't travel due to a hurricane coming in. They'll reschedule or refund, whatever you want. Disney also has a hurricane cancellation policy if your trip is less than 7 days away and the National Hurricane Center [American spelling] at www.nhc.noaa.gov have issued a hurricane warning.

SUNBATHING TIPS

As the Noel Coward song goes: 'Mad dogs and Englishmen go out in the midday sun,' and never a truer word was spoken. Floridians are puzzled by our need to burn ourselves to the crisp as soon as we see the sun, they just don't understand our starvation of it.

But Florida sunshine is deadly for pale white bodies, so take it easy with the sun worshipping. Wear a hat, and as mentioned before, please don't forget about a sun hat for baby. Drink lots of fluids – no, alcohol doesn't count – and splash on the sunscreen, even on cloudy days: at least SPF (SUN PROTECTION FACTOR) 15, although dermatologists recommend SPF 30. Continually reapply every two hours or straight after swimming. Remember to use sun block on tops of feet, ears and backs of legs – three places often forgotten. People who burn their skin in the sun can go on to develop skin cancer, especially those fair-skinned unfortunates. And, if that doesn't scare you enough, 90 percent of premature skin aging (wrinkles, splotches and brown-spots) is caused by sun damage.

TIP Not just for making us look cool, doctors tell us sunglasses (which you'll need all year round in Florida) protect us against cataracts later on in life.

WILDLIFE TIPS

The state of Florida has a varied and interesting wildlife, including alligators, sharks, manatees, bald eagles, blue herons, pelicans, otters, turtles, to name a few.

Alligators: Florida is a land of lakes and swamps inhabited by approximately one million wild adult alligators.

- Alligators aren't as fierce as their cousin the crocodile but have been known to attack small children and pets and sometimes even adults.

- Most lakes have alligators in them. Don't swim in them. Keep away from the shoreline, and especially keep children (and your pets if you live here) out of harm's way.

- It's against the law to feed alligators, as doing so takes away their fear of humans and you could be their next meal. Don't throw anything at them or harass them, either. If you see an alligator in a residential area that could be a harm to humans, call Florida Fish and Wildlife Conservation Commission at Tel: 1-352-732-1225.

Snakes: If you go walking in the woods or long grass, be aware of snakes. Snakebites are rare, but if bitten you should immediately dial emergency telephone number 911 for an ambulance.

Ticks: After a walk in the woods or long grass, do a full body check for ticks (check your children, too). These are nasty insects that burrow into your skin and can cause Lyme disease. If you find one, pull it out immediately with tweezers. If you then discover a rash or have other symptoms such as muscle pain, headache or swollen glands, get medical help immediately. Lyme disease can be fully treated if caught early. Note: For details on other biting insects, go to: Insects in HOLIDAY HOME TIPS chapter on page 31.

Sharks: The Florida coastline is known for sharks but it's unlikely that you'll ever be attacked. When swimming, stay close to the shore in the eye-line of the lifeguard. Don't wear jewellery as sharks are attracted to silver, yellow and gold. And if you see one, stay calm and get out of the water.

Manatees: These gentle giant marine mammals (nickname: sea cows) love to graze vegetation in the warm springs and rivers of Florida. Related to elephants, they are completely harmless  and docile and just like to loll about in the water with their offspring.

TIP Blue Spring Park in OFF THE THEME PARK TRACK chapter on page 134 gives you details on how to see manatees in the wild during November-March.

HEALTH TIPS

Health Insurance: Health travel insurance with a reputable insurance company is probably the wisest investment you'll ever make. Because to require the services of an American hospital when you don't have insurance coverage could well lead you to financial ruin.

True Story: Our children's grandad needed three weeks in hospital in Orlando in two different hospitals, and the final bill for his treatment came to over $140,000. Luckily, he had (annual coverage) holiday health insurance and they paid the bill in full, eventually. At the time (September 2001) his insurance cost him £45. For an extra few pounds it's really worth getting the annual coverage, as this will cover you for any extended hospital treatment, long after the end of your trip.

CULTURE SHOCK TIP

At an American hospital, A&E is called
Emergency or **ER**
(A&E stands for Arts and Entertainment)

Hospital Billing: Have your insurance details ready for the hospital billing department. If you are uninsured, and someone in your family ends up in hospital, always request an ITEMISED INVOICE from the Billing Department of a hospital as they will usually only send you a general one, which doesn't list in detail what medicines and medical services you've been charged for. Check your itemized invoice over, as mistakes are common. Don't be afraid to ask for help deciphering medical terms. If you find a discrepancy, ask for an AUDIT of your hospital bill to be carried out.

Note: Even though upfront hospital discounts are often given to cash payers, uninsured patients can be charged more for medicine, surgeons and other hospital services than insured ones. That's because insurance companies usually negotiate a discount rate with hospitals and not individuals.

Hospital Close To Disney: Celebration Health, 400 Celebration Place, Celebration, 34747. Tel: 407-303-4000.

TIP Don't forget to read your health insurance policy to see what you are covered for, and if you have to declare any pre-existing conditions.

Dentists: If you're unlucky enough to require the services of a dentist, you can either ask your hotel at front desk for a recommendation or telephone the dental referral service at 1-800-DENTIST.

TIP In America, dentists are given the title of doctor.

Doctors: If you need the services of an MD (Medical Doctor, which is the same as our GP) your hotel concierge or guest services may be able to recommend a local one. Otherwise, walk-in clinics are listed in the Yellow Pages under 'Clinics-Medical' (see below for a sample). For any doctor's visit, don't forget to keep all your medical and prescription receipts for claiming on your insurance when you return home. However, if you're admitted into a hospital, the hospital administrators will contact your insurance company for you to make a claim, so just have your insurance details ready.

CULTURE SHOCK TIP

- A doctor's surgery is called a **doctor's office**.
- It's doctor's office hours (not surgery hours).
- Only hospital surgeons use surgeries.

TIP Good news: You don't require any special inoculations to visit the United States.

Accidental Poisoning: If you think you or a family member has been poisoned by something they ingested, then call: Poison Control Telephone Number: 1-800-282-3171.

WALK-IN CLINICS

CENTRA CARE: *Tel: 407-200-CARE (2273) www.CentraCare.org*
There are over 20 Centra Care walk-in doctor's clinics in the Central
Florida area. To find one nearest to you, see list below or go to their
website or call telephone number above. Centra Care also provides
24-hour hotel in-room medical services with free transportation to
any of their clinics. Office hours are between 8.00 AM to 5.00 PM,
Monday through Friday (some clinics are open later, so phone to
check).

Centra Care Walk-In Clinics

Altamonte Springs, Tel: 407-788-2000
Azalea Park, Tel: 407-277-0550
Clermont, Tel: 1-352-394-7757
Colonial Town, Tel: 407-894-3521
Conway, Tel: 407-207-0601
Dr Phillips, Tel: 407-291-9960
Hunter's Creek, Tel: 407-847-6771
Kissimmee, Tel: 407-390-1888
Lake Buena Vista (near Disney), Tel: 407-934-2273
University Blvd., Tel: 407-277-5758
Lee Road, Tel: 407-629-9281
Longwood, Tel: 407-699-8400
Mount Dora, Tel: 1-352-383-6479
Orange Lake, Tel: 407-397-7032
Oviedo, Tel: 407-200-2512
Sanford, Tel: 407-330-3412
Sand Lake, Tel: 407-851-6478
Seminole Towne Center, Tel: 407-330-3412
Waterford Lakes, Tel: 407-381-4810
West Colonial, Tel: 407-296-9096
Wesley Chapel, Tel: 1-813-948-5400
Winter Garden, Tel: 407-654-4965
Winter Park, Tel: 407-677-1140
Winter Park, Lee Road, Tel: 407-629-9281

WALGREEN CLINICS: *www.Walgreens.com/pharmacy*
There are no doctors at Walgreen Walk-in Clinics, but nurse practitioners and physician assistants are on duty. Open: Mon-Fri 8:00 AM to 7:30 PM. Sat-Sun 9:30 AM to 5:00 PM (unavailable at lunch between 1:30-2:30 PM).

Walgreens Walk-In Clinics

7767 W. Irlo Bronson Blvd., Kissimmee, 34747. Tel: 407-390-1701

12100 S. Apopka Vineland Rd., Lake Buena Vista, 32836. Tel: 407-238-0600

8050 International Drive, Orlando, 32819. Tel: 407-352-7071

11600 S. Orange Blossom Trail, Orlando, 32837. Tel: 407-851-8554

408 E. Michigan Street, Orlando, 32806. Tel: 407-843-0956

8000 Lake Underhill Road, Orlando, 32822. Tel: 407-658-1045

701 E. Highway 50, Clermont, 34711. Tel: 352-241-9109

TIP Even though they are called walk-in clinics, it's a good idea to call and make an appointment ahead of time. See 'No Wait Reservations' on their website CentraCare.org

Pharmacies/Drugstores: American pharmacies (which are never known as chemists) are sometimes open 24-hours/7 days a week. The main two pharmacy chains in Orlando are Walgreens and CVS (previously named Eckerd).

TIP Many large supermarkets also have pharmacies.

Pharmacy Open 24-Hours Close To Disney: WALGREENS, *Sat Nav Address: 7767 W. Irlo Bronson Hwy, Kissimmee, 34747 Tel: 407-390-1701.*

DOCTORS ON CALL: *Tel: 407-399-DOCS (3627) www.DoctorsOnCallService.com* For a private doctor's visit to your holiday home or hotel.

WASHROOMS

Toilet is an impolite word in the US. Remember to request the restroom, washroom, bathroom, ladies/gents room. Anything but, 'where's the toilet'.

CULTURE SHOCK TIP

Question: Why don't Americans like the word toilet?

Answer: Much of North America was settled by Puritans, Quakers and other religious groups who didn't like to refer to anything connected to personal bodily functions, so the culture has been handed down.

You won't find public toilets [washrooms] on the high street. You'll find them in restaurants, shopping malls and plazas, hotels, theme parks and visitor centres off the highway. The standard of hygiene is usually high (except maybe at petrol [gas] stations). Many public toilets have hygienic disposable toilet seat covers made from tissue paper, available for use in the stalls. And most have automatic flushes.

TIP As mentioned in the HOLIDAY HOMES chapter, to save precious water, toilets in homes and hotels have smaller pipes, so be careful as they block much easier than British ones and are not designed to flush anything other than toilet tissue.

 ## TELEPHONE TIPS

If you want to purchase a cheap mobile phone [cell phone] for making local calls, you can pick up a pay-as-you-go phone from most supermarkets, pharmacies or phone stores.

Calling Cards: When calling home to Britain, pre-paid calling cards are the cheapest option because hotel phone rates are expensive. You can get these at petrol stations [gas stations], pharmacies, supermarkets, hotels, theme parks and gift stores, etc.

Dialling Tips

- To call home in the UK, dial 011-44 for UK international country code and add your telephone number.
  Important! If you have a 0 at the beginning of your number, do not dial it or you won't get through. For Example: If your number in the UK is 0123-45555, to call home you would dial 011-44-123-45555. Note: Ireland's country code is 353.

- Dialling a mobile phone [cell phone] costs more than dialling a landline.

- In the Orlando/Kissimmee 407 and 321 areas, to call a local number you must include the 407 or 321.

- To call long-distance within the US, preface the number with a 1 (long distance can be as short as in the next town).

- To reverse the charges [call collect]; dial 0 first for the operator.

- People calling you in the US (from the UK) must put a 001 in front of your 10-digit Florida phone number.

Telephone Tip from the People at Disney: To save money when calling Florida from the UK, you can either use Skype or call: Tel: 08448-610-610 and when prompted enter the US telephone number. Calls will cost approximately 1p per minute, which is obviously much cheaper than making a normal international call.

CULTURE SHOCK TIP

\# The hash sign on a phone is called the pound sign.

Free Calls in America: 800, 888, 877 or 888 are all freephone [toll free] numbers. 900 numbers are not free.

Go to: HANDY PHONE NUMBERS & WEBSITES at the end of this book for a list of useful phone numbers.

MAILING LETTERS, POSTCARDS & PARCELS

Letters and Postcards: The post boxes [mailboxes] used for posting [mailing] cards and letters, look like tin bins and are blue coloured, complete with a sign saying UNITED STATES POSTAL SERVICE on them. They have a swing lid you pull down to pop your letters and postcards inside. Hotels, though, will usually mail letters and cards for you. Stamps can be purchased at supermarkets at the checkout as well as post offices. If the post office is closed, then there is usually a stamp machine just outside the building or inside the unlocked lobby. The cost to send an international postcard at time of writing is $1.15. The cost to send a first-class international letter is $3.12. Go to: USPS.com for more information and current prices.

TIP The Mall at Millenia (MallatMillenia.com) shopping mall has a full service post office.

Parcels: You can either use the US Post Office (usps.com/ship/compare-international-services.htm) for sending parcels or go to a FedEx (FedEx.com/us) or UPS Store (UPS.com) (previously called Mailboxes Etc.) or other similar type of office/courier store. Courier stores like UPS will wrap, pack and courier your parcels for you. If you're wrapping them yourself, do not wrap in paper or tie with string; they will not be accepted.

Note: When sending parcels to the UK, it is sometimes cheaper to send them by a courier such as Federal Express (also known as FedEx) than it is to send by the US Post Office (also known as USPS) parcel post, so it's a good idea to get a price comparison.

TIP If you're a Walt Disney World or Universal Resort hotel guest, you can have any purchases you make in the theme parks delivered to your hotel, free of charge.

CULTURE SHOCK TIP

Americans call the postal code the zip code.

WEDDING LOCATIONS

Here's a list of popular spots for weddings that you may want to suggest to your Wedding Planner or you can arrange for yourself…

Walt Disney World (DisneyWeddings.com):
- Wedding Pavilion next door to Disney's Grand Floridian Resort & Spa
- Sea Breeze Point at Disney's Boardwalk Resort
- Wedding Gazebo at Disney's Yacht Club Resort
- Next to Cinderella Castle
- EPCOT World Showcase in one of the 'countries' pavilions

Other Venues not Disney:
- Universal Studios (UOmeetingsandevents.com/On-Site-Hotels/Weddings-Special-Events)
- Harry P. Leu Gardens (LeuGardens.org)
- Kraft Azalea Gardens (CityofWinterPark.org) (up to 20 guests)
- Bok Tower Gardens (BokTowerGardens.org)
- Cypress Grove Park (CypressGroveEstateHouse.com)

Or for the more unusual:
- Hot Air Balloons (Thompsonaire.com)
- Discovery Cove (DiscoveryCove.com)
- Paddlewheel Boat (IndianRiverQueen.com)

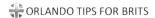
Wedding Planners: Here's a bunch of wedding planners to start you off on your research. All specialise in arranging weddings in Florida for British couples . . .

Get Married in Florida
(GetMarriedinFlorida.com)
Just Marry (JustMarry.com)
Elegant Weddings of Orlando
(ElegantWeddingsofOrlando.com)
Romantic Florida Beach Weddings
(RomanticFloridaBeachWeddings.com)

FLORIDA FAVOURITES

In no particular order, here's a small sample of wonderful things you can do that won't break the bank.

1. Stroll around Disney's Boardwalk lake on a warm Florida evening *(page 57)*.

2. Explore the tropical walkways and atriums of the glass-roofed Gaylord Palms hotel *(pages 18 & 96)*.

3. Dine on a cheese plate and pastry at Les Halles Boulangerie Patisserie in 'France' at EPCOT's World Showcase *(pages 59 & 60)*.

4. 'Fly' over California on the Soarin' ride at EPCOT *(page 61)*.

5. Gain an eye-level view of the giraffes at Brevard Zoo *(page 141)*.

6. Travel to a theme park on a complementary Disney boat *(page 48)*.

7. Sample the international dishes at the annual Food Festival at EPCOT *(page 60)*.

8. Take in the vivid colours and quirky shapes of Islands of Adventure *(page 66)*.

9. Catch the Hogwarts Express steam train and feel like you're in a Harry Potter movie *(page 65)*.

10. Watch best-in-the-world theme-park fireworks any day of the year.

11. Enjoy the exciting Lights, Motors, Action! car stunts at Disney's Hollywood Studios *(page 63)*.

12. Shop in stores that don't close at five *(page 78)*.

13. Fill your tank with petrol [gas] and not need a mortgage.

14. Turn right on a red traffic stop light (when it's safe) *(page 121)*.

15. Convert your British pounds into lots of lovely US dollars *(page 181)*.

16. Enjoy the magic at the The Wizarding World of Harry Potter *(page 66)*.

17. Explore the streets of St. Augustine and feel like you're in old Spain *(page 144)*.

18. Walk into a cool air-conditioned building on a hot, humid day.

19. Drive on wide roads and park in wide car parks *(page 113)*.

20. Shop for a bargain and find two *(page 81)*.

21. Sleep in a big comfortable American king-sized bed.

22. Jump on the rides when everyone else is watching the fireworks.

23. Enjoy a big salad at Sweet Tomatoes *(page 95)*.

24. Walk past long queues in the free FASTPASS+ line at Disney parks *(page 47)*.

25. Take a free Disney monorail for no particular reason *(page 11)*.

26. Drive on the beach at Daytona *(page 138)*.

27. Hangout in Celebration, the Disney-designed town *(page 143)*.

28. Be a kid again, any time you want.

29. Explore the African-themed ground floor [first floor] of Animal Kingdom Lodge *(page 64)*.

30. Watch silverback gorillas being mischievous at Disney's Animal Kingdom *(page 63)*.

31. Wind down a lazy river ride on an inflatable tube *(page 73)*.

32. Eat a slice of pizza while people watching at Universal CityWalk (pages *55 & 82)*.

33. See the wild manatees at Blue Spring Park *(page 134)*.

34. Ride the Spider-man ride at Islands of Adventure *(page 67)*.

35. Dive into a cool, refreshing swimming pool at the end of a long, hot day.

Start your list here . . .

_____

_____

BRITISH/AMERICAN WORDS

We may know the meaning of many American words and sayings from watching films or TV. And Americans love our words like fortnight and smashing. But you'll probably be met with a blank stare if you ask for a plaster or an off-licence or a flannel. So, in the following table are words you could encounter to discover that Britain and America have some very different ways of saying things.

BRITISH	AMERICAN	NOTES
Aeroplane	Airplane	
Aubergine	Eggplant	
Autumn	Fall	
Balaclava	Ski Mask	
Bath	Bathtub	
Beach Hut	Cabana	
Bed Settee	Sofa Bed	*or pull-out bed or rollaway bed or murphy Bed*
Beetroot	Beets	
Bill (The)	Check (The)	*in a restaurant*
Bin Bag/Liner	Trash Bag/Garbage Bag	
Biro	Ball Point Pen	
Biscuits	Cookies	*biscuits are similar to savoury scones (buttered or served with gravy)*
Bonnet	Hood	*'Take a look under the hood'*
Boot	Trunk	

BRITISH	AMERICAN	NOTES
Braces	Suspenders	*braces are for teeth*
Bum Bag	Fanny Pack	
Bumper	Fender	*a rear-end bump is called a fender bender*
Camper Van	Conversion Van	
Candy Floss	Cotton Candy	
Car Hire	Car Rental	
Car Park	Parking Lot	
Caravan	Trailer	
Carpet (not fitted)	Rug	
Cashpoint	ATM or Cash Machine	
Casualty	Emergency Room (ER)	*or just Emergency*
Central Reservation	Median	
Chemist	Pharmacy or Drugstore	*Walgreens or CVS chains*
Chips	French Fries	*or just fries*
Choc-Ice	Klondike Bar	
Cinema/Pictures	Movie Theatre(er)	*or Multiplex*

BRITISH	AMERICAN	NOTES
Clothes Peg	Clothes Pin	
Cooker	Stove	
Cot	Crib	*a cot is a small collapsible or folding bed*
Courgettes	Zucchini	
Crisps	Chips	
Curtains	Drapes	*curtains understood*
Cutlery	Silverware	
Dear (as in cost)	Expensive	
Dialling Code	Area Code	
Diversion	Detour	
Doctor's Surgery	Doctor's Office	*a doctor is also known as an MD or physician*
Dog Lead	Dog Leash	
Double Cream	Heavy or Whipping Cream	*but 'Half and Half' is half milk, half cream for your coffee*
Dual Carriageway	Multi-lane Highway	*or divided highway*
Dummy	Pacifier	

BRITISH	AMERICAN	NOTES
Dungarees	Overalls	*Dungarees are a brand of jeans*
Dustbin	Garbage/Trash Bin	*'The garbage truck will take your trash'*
Duvet/Eiderdown	Comforter/Quilt	
Enter/Exit Slip Road	On-Ramp/Off-Ramp	
Estate Agent	Realtor	*or Real Estate Agent*
Exhaust Pipe	Tailpipe	
Fish Fingers	Fish Sticks	
Fitted Wardrobe	Closet	
Flannel	Washcloth/Facecloth	
Flat	Apartment	*say 'for rent' or 'to lease' instead of 'to let'*
Flyover	Overpass	
Folding Bed	Cot	*a cot is called a crib*
Football	Soccer	*football is game similar to rugby called American football*
Fortnight	Two Weeks	
Freephone	Toll Free	
Fringe (as in hair)	Bangs	*'I need my bangs trimmed'*

BRITISH	AMERICAN	NOTES
Full Board	American Plan (AP)	
Gammon	Cured Ham	
Garden	Back or Front Yard	*a garden in the US is either a vegetable plot or a flowerbed*
Give Way	Yield	
Granny Flat	Mother-in-law apartment	
Greengrocer	Produce section of a supermarket	*pronounced pro-doos*
Grill	Broil	*grill understood*
Half Board	Modified American Plan (MAP)	
Hand Brake	Emergency Brake	
Head Waiter	Maître d'	
High-heeled shoes	Pumps	
Hole in the Wall/ Cash Point	Cash Machine/ATM	
Holiday	Vacation	*a holiday usually refers to a Public Holiday such as Christmas*
Housing Estate	Sub-division	*housing estate understood*
Ice-lolly	Popsicle	

BRITISH	AMERICAN	NOTES
Identification (for alcohol, clubs, bars, banks, etc.)	ID	*Passport or Driver's License*
Indicators	Turn Signals	*or blinkers*
Jacket Potato	Baked Potato	
Jam	Jelly or Jam	*PB&J sandwich is a peanut butter and jelly (jam) sandwich*
Jelly	Jell-O	
Joint (of meat)	Roast or Pot Roast	
Jumper	Sweater	*a jumper is a sleeveless dress worn over a blouse or sweater (or a baby's outfit with bib top)*
Junction	Intersection	
Knickers	Panties	*or underwear*
Lycra	Spandex	
Lard	Shortening	
Launderette	Laundromat	
Lay-by	Rest Area or Rest Stop	

BRITISH	AMERICAN	NOTES
Lemonade Pop/ Fizzy Lemonade	Sprite or 7-UP	*lemonade in the US is the old-fashioned type made with real lemons*
Lift	Elevator	*there's no ground floor marked on an elevator; this is called the first floor*
Lilo	Air Mattress	
Liver Sausage	Liverwurst	
Lolly or Lollypop	Sucker	
Loo (as in toilet)	John (slang)	
Lorry	Truck	*articulated lorries are called tractor trailers*
Mac or Macintosh	Raincoat	
Madeira Cake	Pound Cake	*similar to*
Manual Gear Box	Standard Shift or Stick Shift	
Midges (that bite)	No-see-ums	*they can even squeeze through fly screens*
Mince meat	Ground Beef	*or hamburger meat*
Mineral Water	Bottled Water	

BRITISH	AMERICAN	NOTES
Mobile Phone	Cell Phone	
Motorway	Interstate, Highway or Freeway	
Multi-storey Car Park	Multi-level Parking Garage	
Nappy	Diaper	
Naught/Nought (as in 0)	Zero or O	
Note (as in money)	Bill (as in dollar bill)	
Number Plate	License Plate or Tag	
Off-licence	Liquor Store	
Pavement	Sidewalk	*a pavement is a road or any paved area*
People Carrier	Minivan	
Petrol	Gas or Gasoline	
Petrol Station	Gas Station	*or service station*
Pitch and Putt	Miniature Golf	
Plain Flour	All-purpose Flour	
Plaster	Band-aid	
Polo Neck	Turtle Neck	

BRITISH	AMERICAN	NOTES
Pop (as in drink of)	Soda	
Porridge	Oatmeal	
Post Box	Mailbox	*mail a letter, not post it*
Pram	Baby Carriage	
Purse	Wallet	*a purse is a handbag*
Pushchair	Stroller	
Queue	Line-up	
Reception	Front Desk	
Receptionist	Desk Clerk	*pronounced clerk not clark*
Reverse (telephone) Charges	Call Collect	
Ring Road	Beltway	
Rock (seaside)	Stick Candy	
Roundabout	Traffic Circle	*or rotary*
Rubbish	Garbage or Trash	*rubbish understood though*
Runner Beans	Green Beans/String Beans	

BRITISH	AMERICAN	NOTES
Salad Cream	Mayonnaise/Mayo	
Salt Cellar	Salt Shaker	
Sandpit	Sandbox	
Sellotape	Scotch Tape	
Serviette	Napkin	
Settee	Couch	*also sofa or loveseat*
Shopping Trolley	Shopping Cart	
Shops	Stores, Shopping Plazas, Malls, Strip Malls	*shops understood*
Single Ticket	One Way Ticket	
Skimmed Milk	Skim Milk or 2% Milk	
Slip Road	Ramp	*off ramp or on ramp*
Solicitor	Lawyer	*a solicitor in the US is someone that seeks trade or contributions*
Spot (on skin)	Zit or Pimple	
Spring Onion	Green Onion/ Scallion	
Squash (drink)	Concentrated Juice	*American children often have Kool-Aid or juice boxes*

BRITISH	AMERICAN	NOTES
Starters	Appetizers	
Still Drinks	Non-carbonated	
Stock Cube (OXO)	Bouillon Cube	
Stopover	Layover	
Suspenders	Garters	*or garter belt*
Sweets	Candy	*sweets are desserts*
Swimming Costume	Swimsuit	
Swiss Roll	Jelly Roll	
Takeaway	Takeout/To Go	*'Is that for here or to go?'*
Tap	Faucet	*but say tap water not faucet water*
Taxi Rank	Taxi Stand	
Tea Towel	Dish Towel	
Teat (as in baby's bottle teat)	Nipple	
Tights	Pantyhose	*tights are the thick type usually worn by dancers or children*

BRITISH	AMERICAN	NOTES
Tin (as in tin of soup)	Can	*can opener not tin opener, canned tomatoes not tinned*
Toilet	Washroom, Restroom or Bathroom	*or sometimes powder room*
Toll Road	Turnpike	
Torch	Flash Light	
Trainers	Sneakers	
Trousers	Pants	*trousers understood (lady's trouser suit known as pant suit*
Turn-ups	Cuffs	
Van	Pick-Up	
Verge	Hard Shoulder	
Vest	Undershirt	*a vest is a waistcoat*
Wardrobe	Closet	*wardrobe understood though*
Wash-up	Wash hands	
Washing-up Liquid	Dish Soap	*not to be confused with dish washer soap*

BRITISH	AMERICAN	NOTES
Wellington Boots	Rubber Boots	
Windscreen	Windshield	
Zebra Crossing	Crosswalk/Pedestrian Crossing	

THEME PARK SNAPSHOT

So you're in a hurry and you and your family can't decide which theme park to go to today. Here's a sum-up of the major Orlando parks to help you all decide. (See Theme Parks section on page 58 for full descriptions.)

MAGIC KINGDOM: The one with rides suitable for young children, such as Peter Pan's Flight, Seven Dwarfs Mine Train and family-friendly roller coasters like Splash Mountain.

EPCOT: The one with all the replica countries at World Showcase, such as France and Italy and Mexico and England (and mostly mild rides), but also where there's a section called Future World and intense ride Mission: Space.

HOLLYWOOD STUDIOS: The one that used to be called MGM Studios, with all the movie- and TV-based rides and shows, such as Indiana Jones Epic Stunt Spectacular and car-stunt show Lights, Motors, Action! And not-for-the-faint-of-heart Twilight Zone Tower of Terror.

ANIMAL KINGDOM: The wildlife one with real animals such as silverback gorillas, and the occasional ride such as Expedition Everest – Legend of the Forbidden Mountain.

UNIVERSAL STUDIOS: The one with rides based on blockbuster movies, such as Men in Black, Transformers and Revenge of the Mummy. Diagon Alley is here with Escape from Gringots ride (riders must be 42" tall) and Hogwarts Express train to take you to Universal's Islands of Adventure where the main part of the Harry Potter world is (you'll need a 2-park ticket for the train).

ISLANDS OF ADVENTURE: The colourful one run by Universal, where you'll find The Wizarding World of Harry Potter, The Amazing Adventures of Spider-man ride, Dr Seuss's The Cat in the Hat, Jurassic Park, and where inside Marvel Super Hero island there's a super fast roller coaster called Incredible Hulk.

SEAWORLD: The one with marine shows, featuring whales and dolphins, plus a few rides including the fast, floorless roller coaster Kraken.

DISCOVERY COVE: The exclusive one where you can swim with dolphins and lie on a tropical beach all day (no rides).

AIRPORTS: Orlando International Airport: Flights – Tel: 407-825-TIME (8463) General – 407-825-2001 www.OrlandoAirports.net **Sanford Airport:** Tel: 407-585-4000 www.OrlandoSanfordAirport.com

BUS SERVICE: Tel: 407-841-LYNX (5969) www.GoLynx.com

BUSCH GARDENS: Tickets: 1-888-800-5447 www.BuschGardens.com (click on Tampa)

DISNEY WORLD: Animal Kingdom, Hollywood Studios, Magic Kingdom, EPCOT (https://Disneyworld.disney.go.com)

- DISNEY UK Tel: 0870-242-4900 https://disneyworld.disney.go.com/help/phone

- DISNEY DINING Tel: 407-WDW-DINE (939-3463) UK Tel: 0800-169-0748 https://disneyworld.disney.go.com/dining/#/reservations-accepted

- DISNEY GOLF Tel: 407-WDW-GOLF (939-4653)

- DISNEY EVENTS/TOURS Tel: 407-WDW-TOUR (939-8687) https://disneyworld.disney.go.com/events-tours

- DISNEY TICKETS Tel: 407-824-4321 UK Tel: 0800-169-0743 www.DisneyWorld.com (click link for UK International Version). See also T below for Theme Park discount tickets

Note: See W below for Disney's Water Parks

DISCOVERY COVE: Tel: 407-370-1280 www.DiscoveryCove.com (or for Brits: www.SeaWorldParks.co.uk)

DIRECTORY ENQUIRIES: Tel: 411

DOCTORS at the Centra Care Walk-in urgent care clinics run by Florida Hospitals (over 20 locations): Tel: 407-200-CARE (2273) (ask for clinic closest to your hotel or holiday home) www.CentraCare.org

DOCTORS ON CALL: Tel: 407-399-DOCS (3627) www.DoctorsOnCallService.com

DISNEY SPRINGS (formerly Downtown Disney): Tel: 407-WDW-MAGIC (939-6244) www.DownTownDisney.com (click on Walt Disney World)

EMERGENCIES: fire, police, ambulance (no coins required for public phone) Tel: 911

FLORIDA STATE PARKS: Tel: 1-850-245-2157 www.FloridaStateParks.org

INTERNATIONAL DRIVE:

- I-RIDETROLLEY BUS (stopping at shops and entertainment) Tel: 407-354-5656 www.IrideTrolley.com
- I-DRIVE INFORMATION (shopping, entertainment and hotels) www.InternationalDriveOrlando.com

ISLANDS OF ADVENTURE: Tel: 407-363-8000 (ask for information on Islands of Adventure) www.UniversalOrlando.com

LOST AND FOUND:

- Lost and Found MAGIC KINGDOM, ANIMAL KINGDOM & HOLLYWOOD STUDIOS Tel: 407-824-4245
- Lost and Found EPCOT Tel: 407-560-7500
- Lost and Found UNIVERSAL STUDIOS Tel: 407-224-4244
- Lost and Found SEAWORLD Tel: 407-363-2400 (Guest Services)
- Lost and Found Islands of Adventure Tel: 407-224-4245

PUSHCHAIR [STROLLER] RENTAL:

- BABY'S AWAY Tel: 407-334-0232 www.BabysAway.com
- KINGDOM STROLLERS Tel: 407-674-1866 KingdomStrollers.com

SEAWORLD: US Tel: 407-351-3600 UK Tel: 0800-231-5281 www.SeaWorldParks.com or www.SeaWorldParks.co.uk

Note: For Aquatica see Water Parks below

SPORTS: ESPN Wide World of Sports Tel: 407-939-4263 www.DisneyWorldSports.com

TAXI CABS:

- QUICK TRANSPORTATION Tel: 407-354-2456 or 1-888-784-2522 www.QuickTransportation.com

- CENTURY EXPRESS Tel: 407-505-6352 or 1-877-250-4585 www.CenturyExpress.com

- QUICKSILVER TAXIS Tel: 407-299-1434 or 1-888-GO-TO-WDW (468-6939) www.QuickSilver-tours.com/services.asp

- MEARS TRANSPORTATION Tel: 407-422-2222 or Orlando Airport Shuttle: 407-423-5566 www.MearsTransportation.com/taxi-services

TIP For groups of 5 passengers or more, ask for a taxi van.

TOURIST INFORMATION:

- VISIT ORLANDO (the Official Tourism Office) Tel: 407-363-5872 or 1-800-972-3304 www.VisitOrlando.com

- TOURIST INFORMATION KISSIMMEE Tel: 407-742-8200 www.ExperienceKissimmee.com

THEME PARK TICKETS (DISCOUNT)

- ATTRACTION TICKETS DIRECT UK Tel: 0845-130-3876 or 0800-086-1699 www.Attraction-Tickets-Direct.co.uk

- FLORIDATIX UK Tel: 0800-980-5552 www.Floridatix.co.uk

- UNDERCOVER TOURIST: UK Tel: 0800-081-1702 or US Tel: 1-800-846-1302 www.UndercoverTourist.com

THEME PARK NEWS BLOG: www.OrlandoParksNews.blogspot.com

UNIVERSAL STUDIOS: Guest Services – Tel: 407-224-4233, General Number – Tel: 407-363-8000 www.UniversalOrlando.com

UNIVERSAL DINING RESERVATIONS: Tel: 407-224-4012

UNIVERSAL CITYWALK: Tel: 407-224-2690 www.CityWalkOrlando.com

TIP When dialling within the area of Orlando you must include the 407 area code. If outside of Orlando but still in the US, preface with a 1.

WATER PARKS:

- Disney's Blizzard Beach Tel: 407-939-7812
  https://Disneyworld.disney.go.com/destinations/Blizzard-beach

- Disney's Typhoon Lagoon Tel: 407-560-4141
  https://Disneyworld.disney.go.com/destinations/Typhoon-lagoon

- SeaWorld's Aquatica Tel: 407-351-3600
  www.SeaWorldParks.co.uk or www.SeaWorldAquatica.com

TIP For calling US cheaply Tel: 08448-610-610 (when prompted enter US telephone number). Calls cost approximately 1p per minute.

WEATHER: Tel: 321-255-0212 (ext. 412) www.Weather.com

WHEELCHAIR RENTAL:

- Walker Mobility Tel: 407-518-6000 or 1-888-726-6837
  www.WalkerMobility.com

- Scoot Around Tel: 1-888-441-7575 www.ScootAround.com

TIP If dialling an Orlando number from the UK: place 001 in front of the phone number (except for American 800 or other toll-free numbers, which don't work from the UK).

RESTAURANTS, CAFES & PUBS
PHONE NUMBERS & WEBSITES

Note: Go to DINING OUT TIPS chapter on page 85 for full details of the eateries below.

Aashirwad (Indian): Tel: 407-370-9830 www.AashirwadRestaurant.com

Bahama Breeze: www.BahamaBreeze.com

- International Drive – Tel: 407-248-2499

- Vineland Avenue – Tel: 407-938-9010

- Kissimmee – Tel: 407-390-0353

DISNEY DINING: US Tel: 407-WDW-DINE (939-3463)
UK Disney Dining Tel: 0800-169-0748
https://disneyworld.disney.go.com/help/dining-reservations

Ethos (Vegan): Tel: 407-228-3898 www.EthosVeganKitchen.com

Fiddler's Green Irish Pub & Eatery: Tel: 407-645-2050
www.FiddlersGreenOrlando.com

Garden Cafe: Tel: 407-999-9799 (no website).

George and Dragon Pub: Tel: 407-351-3578
www.OrlandoGeorgeandDragon.com

Harp and Celt Irish Pub & Restaurant: Tel: 407-481-2928
www.HarpandCelt.com

Kim Wu Chinese Restaurant: Tel: 407-293-0752 (no website).

Magnolia Terrace Tea Room & Restaurant: Tel: 1-352-556-4819
www.MagnoliaTerraceTearoom.com

Mellow Mushroom: Orlando Tel: 407-384-4455
https://MellowMushroom.com/store/orlando
Winter Park Tel: 407-657-7755
https://MellowMushroom.com/store/winter-park

Memories of India: Tel: 407-370-3277 www.MemoriesofIndiaCuisine.com

New Punjab Restaurant (Indian): Tel: 407-352-7887
www.NewPunjabIndian.com

New York China Buffet: Tel: 407-238-9198 (no website).

Park Plaza Gardens Restaurant: Tel: 407-645-2475
http://parkplazagardens.com/high-tea-champagne-on-the-avenue

Ponderosa Steakhouse: www.PonderosaSteakHouses.com

- 6362 International Drive – Tel: 407-352-9343
- 8510 International Drive – Tel: 407-354-1477
- Kissimmee 34747 – Tel: 407-396-7721
- Kissimmee 34746 – Tel: 407-397-2100

Power House Cafe Tel: 407-645-3616 www.PowerHouseCafe.com

Raglan Road Irish Pub & Restaurant: Tel: 407-938-0300
www.RaglanRoad.com

Sweet Tomatoes: Kissimmee Tel: 407-465-0023, 4678 East Colonial Drive, Orlando Tel: 407-896-8770; 12561 S. Apopka-Vineland Road, Orlando Tel: 407-938-9461; International Festival, 6877 South Kirkman Road Tel: 407-363-3636 www.Souplantation.com

Tabla Bar and Grill (Indian): Tel: 407-248-9400 www.Tablabar.com

Taste of Punjab (Indian): Tel: 407-507-3900 www.TasteofPunjabOrlando.com

The Boheme Restaurant (Grand Bohemian Hotel for Afternoon Tea): Tel: 407-313-9000 www.GrandBohemianHotel.com

The Lobby Lounge (Ritz-Carlton Hotel for Afternoon Tea): Tel: 407-393-4034 www.GrandeLakes.com

The Pub Orlando: Tel: 407-352-2305 www.ExperienceThePub.com/Orlando

---

UNIVERSAL DINING: Tel: 407-224-4012 www.UniversalOrlando.com

Veggie Garden: Tel: 407-228-1740 www.VeggieGardenVegan.com

Wild Rice Buffet: Tel: 407-628-0088 www.WildRiceBuffet.com

Woodlands (Indian): Tel: 407-854-3330 www.WoodlandsUSA.com

AIRLINE
PHONE NUMBERS & WEBSITES

AIRLINE	PHONE UK	PHONE USA	WEB
American Airlines	0844-499-7300	1-800-433-7300	AA.com
British Airways	0844-493-0787	1-800-AIRWAYS	BritishAirways.com
Delta/KLM Airlines	0871-221-1222	1-800-241-4141	Delta.com
US Airways	0845-600-3300	1-800-428-4322	USAirways.com
United Airlines	0845-607-6760	1-800-525-0280	United.com
Virgin Atlantic	0844-209-7777	1-800-862-8621	Virgin-Atlantic.com

Have a wonderful time in Orlando *!*

Printed in Great Britain
by Amazon

82475445R00139